LOVE IS THE ANSWER

Homilies of Father Greg Tolaas
Ordinary Time 2001

2011

Table of Contents

Preface

Father Greg Tolaas

Like the sunflower,
you possess a coffee-ground earthy heart.
Centered, grounded, sturdy-stemmed,
your soul certain to whom it belongs.

Awaiting again to hear
your compelling words,
firing from the pulpit
like feisty goldenrod sunflower petals
that push and prod "do more,"
you breathe the value of time
and cannot bear a wasted grain.

You call us "Be the body of Christ" —
Physically, mentally, spiritually, emotionally —
intolerant of substandard performance,
for the need is NOW:
Mentor that child! Coach basketball!
Make donuts! Live Peace! Speak Justice!
Love Neighbors! Serve with joy!
Serve until empty. God will fill you!

You emulate the head of the church, Christ,
candidly sharing feelings, thoughts, strengths,
weaknesses,
acknowledging your energy sputters and spews
like earthly prayer,
but remains tethered firmly to the Lord's will
and ways.

Please know, heaven-sent man,
that we need your continued guidance
and persistent "kicks in the pants."
Agreed, at times we are afraid and lazy
and weak,
yet also compassionate and caring and together
very strong.
*So grateful are we Philipians for who you've
helped us become.*

—Sheila Gales Biernat

Written for Fr. Greg during his final hospitalization.

Forward

Pay attention! … Love radically! … Give your bulletin a careful read. …

For anyone who knew Father Greg Tolaas, or even if you knew someone that knew Father Greg Tolaas, these are words that likely strike a spiritual chord with you. His words would resonate with you for hours, days, even years, and most of his teachings could be whittled down to a few key messages. Those who had the opportunity to experience him, first hand, have likely had the gift of this wisdom left on their hearts and in their souls.

September 7, [2010] marked the seventh anniversary of Greg's passing from this world, to the next. I had thought about this over the summer, because you see, September 7 also marked the first day I would return to full-time teaching in a first grade classroom after having been on leave for five years. Despite the busyness of summer winding down and the school year starting up, I had realized I would make this transition on a day that, seven years ago, brought a lot of transition. However, what I didn't realize is that I'd be standing here, doing this, today.

About a week and a half ago, I was down on the computer, spending an evening like I had been spending almost every evening these days, working hard on more school stuff, after having spent about twelve hours in my classroom preparing during the day, coming home and doing dinner, getting the boys to whatever activity was going on that evening, doing bedtime for them, and then getting back to work on more school stuff – until way too late. And Scott, as an administrator, was up to his elbows in all the beginning of the year stuff, too. So, at about 11:00 p.m. this particular night, I noticed an email from Father Jules to our family and the Theisen family, asking us if we could prepare something for the homily for Greg's memorial mass as well as a meditation for the bulletin, since we had known him in person. Well, I was very busy. I knew that I could not do this. I had a classroom to set up, first graders to meet, my own children to prepare, lessons to plan, and I knew that the PTO newsletter was not going to write itself by the first day of school. Father Jules must not have realized the time of year it is and he must not realize the amount of stress teachers and administrators are under this time of year, not to mention the stress of change our family would walk through in the upcoming days. Besides, if you need someone in front of a group of first graders, I'm your girl, but someone to address the parish? Not so much. I knew I would have a conversation with Julia [Theisen] about this, it seemed likely that this whole request would just default to her. After all, anyone who was here on Mother's Day knows what a gifted speaker she is as she shared her motherly wisdom with us that day. She would really be the likely candidate if anyone from the Johnson or Theisen family was going to do this. So, I knew I'd respectfully decline this offer to Father Jules at some point, but in the meantime, I just quietly dismissed it, because I had some really pressing school things to keep working on.

The next night on my drive home from school at about 7:30, I was in touch with Julia to figure out how we were going to figure this out (and she, by the way, was telling me that this was much too late to be leaving school and that it could not continue and that she would be checking in with me on that and calling me on it if it did continue.) She, though, mid-conversation, said, "Wait, what weekend is that? We are supposed to be out of town with Jay's family that weekend."

It just stopped me in my tracks. I remember saying, "Well, what am I supposed to do?" She helped me think through the words I could say to Father Jules to decline his request for me to speak, because it really was a difficult time of the year for our family.

So, I composed an email to send to Jules, but just saved it

to send in the morning.

Then, the next morning, to put it in Greg's words, "In walks my shower."

If I shed tears before the beginning of the school year, it typically has something to do with my overwhelming feelings and anxiety I have about the start of the year. But this morning, my tears in the shower were not related to school; I could easily feel that. They were about Greg, about how much I still love him, how much I miss him, and about how strongly he has impacted our lives … even still. He walked me through my own spiritual struggles when Scott and I met; do I stay Lutheran, or do I become Catholic? And when I decided to become Catholic, he, with Scott's support as my sponsor, lead me through the RCIA process. He officiated our wedding at the University of St. Thomas, he baptized our first baby – here. He taught us to be still and listen, to breathe and how to appreciate the miracle of every single breath we take. He was gentle, loving, and kind. He taught us that much prayer means much power, little prayer means little power, and no prayer means no power, and he was really hard on us.

That was it right there. That was the thought that caught me off guard in the shower that morning. I was brought back to the feelings I had sitting in the pews near the back of the church, where on many a Sunday, Greg would call us to participate. It would begin at the beginning of Mass as we were invited, no, we were instructed, "as it is a custom, here at St. Philip, to greet one another." And it wasn't good enough to turn to those around you, you had to get out of your pew and walk over to someone you did not know and introduce yourself.

It seems funny to me now, but at the time, that was out of my comfort zone. But then, later in the Mass, he would call us to participate even further: during the week, outside of church, fully participate in some kind of service. He made us reflect upon how we were, if we were, inviting God into our lives – moving us to continue to step out of that comfort zone, to forget about the "blah blah blah, now back to me" that you had going on in your life.

Of course, most Sundays I felt pretty guilty because I knew there was no way I was doing enough. But I was really busy – we were both working full time and it takes a lot of energy to be elementary school teachers, and we had a new baby at home, and then there was the drive – we had more of a drive.

Hmmmm, those excuses, as I remembered them in the

shower that morning, were sounding a little familiar to me. And I realized right there in the shower, that I was being called to participate. And that this was my work – not Julia's, not Scott's, not whoever Father Jules might need to find to take our place, but this was my work.

And I realized that this was so much of what Greg stood for. Pay attention and get out of your pew and participate. Do something!

If you did not know Father Greg personally, he was a beautiful, brilliant, and amazing person. He was beautiful on the inside and the outside. During his time as the head of campus ministry at the University of St. Thomas, I think he was even called "Father What-a-Waste" by many a female student.

Brilliant! He was so smart, he watched documentaries, he read everything, travelled extensively, from his beginnings he was well educated, and he tapped into the experiences of others in a way that brought him so much wisdom and connection to the big picture. He really was amazing. He was amazing because at first glance, when he was shaking us up, calling us out of our pews, you might think "easy for you to say, beautiful, brilliant, and amazing man already blessed by God in so many ways." But once you got to know him, you'd see that he had faced many a hardship and challenge in his life, physically, emotionally, and spiritually.

You see, Greg was born with cystic fibrosis, as were several of his siblings (there were six kids in his family). CF affects your lungs and fills them with mucous making it hard to breathe, requiring treatments every day, not to mention a variety of medications. Greg's reliance on others to help with treatments was a humbling experience for him. He would talk about receiving his First Communion early, in the first grade, instead of the second grade. While he thought it was just because he was special, it was really because they thought he wouldn't be alive in second grade. He was almost denied ordination, again, because he just wasn't expected to live that long.

When Greg did a Mass here, we were often blessed by his beautiful voice – really truly beautiful voice, especially in song. And we were boldly told that we were not welcome to come to St. Philip to "get our share of Greg." But let's be honest, that voice during the Eucharistic prayer some mornings is what got me there! Greg would sing, the choir would join in for parts, and the assembly would also have its part in singing this prayer. It was communion at its finest – a real trinity!

What many didn't know, though, was how much physical energy, how many pills and treatments it took in those last masses to get him to be able to enrich our mass in this way, and how much it completely exhausted his physical energy.

Later in life, Greg became diabetic, and in the last years of life, suffered from kidney problems and underwent dialysis about four days a week. He was in line for lung and kidney transplants and was granted those in June of 2003. Although the transplants went well, he did not leave the hospital as he did not recover from infection that set in after the surgeries.

Emotionally, Greg had more than his share of tribulation. He watched siblings suffer and die from cystic fibrosis. He was only ten when his mother died in childbirth. His grandmother took on the maternal role for most of his life. Spiritually, Greg met many a struggle. One that I think of is his calling to St. Philip. He left a thriving and comfortable community as the head of Campus Ministry at the University of St. Thomas, where he was loved and admired, working with college students – many of whom were, for the most part, from fairly affluent families. He came to a dying parish of St. Philip, in a struggling neighborhood community and faced many challenges as he engendered true compassion, outreach, and social justice, knowing he was really rocking the boat with every change he offered. So, any time I would have my excuses and limitations, I would only have to think of Greg's life, and then try to reflect upon why it is that I can't do what I think I might be called to do in my little corner of the world.

Despite my early hesitation, I am grateful to be here with you today, and I am honored to speak about a man who brought so many blessings to my life. As we remember and honor Father Greg today, and reflect upon his deep faith, his radical love, his beautiful voice and words, I invite you this week to pay attention to how you are called to participate. Pay attention to how that calling might be hidden – how you might be covering it up with your busyness and all the really important things you think you need to do. Pay attention to how you can make room in your life for God and for what you are called by Him to do.

Heidi M. Johnson

Acknowledgements

Father Greg Tolaas's homilies were filled with love. Everyone who knew Greg kept his endearing messages in their hearts. He urged us to "Let love meet love." And "Err on the side of love." Also, we were instructed that "Love is the Answer."

We lovingly pay attention to those who helped us on this journey of love.

To Lee O'Daniel for recording the original homilies of Father Greg and preparing them for production.

To Betty Lou Miller for typing each homily from the CDs.

To Michael Benham for putting the book together from front to back cover, paginating, photos and any other of the myriad jobs involved in getting camera-ready copy.

To Tim Montgomerey for designing the front cover, sales flyers, and CD covers.

To Fred Miller for use of his extraordinary photo for the book cover.

To Brian Mogren for the book's photos.

To Michael Benham for the final page photo of his Uncle Dale, the Deacon of St. Philip.

To Betty Lou Miller, and Don and Donna Montgomery for editing the book.

Coordinated by Donna Montgomery.

To Our Generous Donors (alphabetically):

Arch and Barbara Benham
Brendan and Miaja Cassidy
Gail Gebo
Scott and Heidi Johnson
John and Nancy Jurkovich
Barbara Korman
Arlene Mogren
Rose Mary Mundahl
Clarence Shallbetter

Dedication

**Dedicated to all who believe love is the answer,
and then act in non-violent and peaceful ways.**

Father Gregory Robert Tolaas
Born March 27, 1956 –
Born to Eternal Life September 7, 2003

**Priest of the Archdiocese of
Saint Paul and Minneapolis**
May 28, 1983 to September 7, 2003

Pastor of The Church of St. Philip
August 1997 to September 7, 2003

After Mass one Sunday, I asked Father Greg if he was recording his homilies. He said, "No, Why?" I replied that they were far too big for just our parish. A few weeks later, he told me his homilies were now being recorded. I feel Greg, at that time, realized his homilies must be shared with many, therefore giving us his blessing to share them with you.

We hope you feel as blessed to hear his words as we feel blessed to bring them to you.

Donna Montgomery

Chapter 1

10th Sunday of Ordinary Time, June 10, 2001

Trinity Sunday

We learned today in the word of God that Wisdom is talking to us; and Wisdom is one of the faces of God. And Wisdom is saying, 'I created you. I am the creativity and the imagination that made the world beautiful with every flower and the seas and the mountains. I'm the one who gave you imagination. I'm the one who leads you to joy. And I, Wisdom, look at you and I take delight, I take delight in you.'

- Father Greg Tolaas

Gospel

Luke 7:1-10

[1] When Jesus had finished saying all these things to the people, he went to Capernaum. [2] A Roman officer there had a servant who was very dear to him; the man was sick and about to die. [3] When the officer heard about Jesus, he sent some Jewish elders to ask him to come and heal his servant. [4] They came to Jesus and begged him earnestly, "This man really deserves your help. [5] He loves our people and he himself built a synagogue for us."

[6] So Jesus went with them. He was not far from the

house when the officer sent friends to tell him, "Sir, don't trouble yourself. I do not deserve to have you come into my house, [7] neither do I consider myself worthy to come to you in person. Just give the order, and my servant will get well. [8] I, too, am a man placed under the authority of superior officers, and I have soldiers under me. I order this one, "Go!' and he goes; I order that one, 'Come!' and he comes; and I order my slave, 'Do this!' and he does it."

[9] Jesus was surprised when he heard this; he turned around and said to the crowd following him, "I tell you, I have never found faith like this, not even in Israel!"

[10] The messengers went back to the officer's house and found his servant well.

Homily

Do I see Reme back there? Reme, are you here? Is your mother here? She is? Okay, Reme's mother is from the Ivory Coast and she speaks only French.

(Bienven nous sommes trés heureux que vous êtes ici aujourd'hui, bienvenue. Je suis désolé de dire que je parle un peu seulement le Francais. Je parlerais en Anglais. Je suis désolé.)

Welcome, we are truly pleased to have you here with us today. Welcome. I apologize, but I am not fluent in French. I will be speaking in English; I am sorry. Let's welcome her today.

I went yesterday to the 75th vow of Sister Mary Regina about whom I said a sentence last week and about whom I wrote in the bulletin the week before. I have known her for twenty-five years. Unless you have a stingy heart, or a jealous heart, I don't think you can encounter her and not like her. I don't think you can encounter this tiny woman in her black and white habit from the 16th century, whose eyes are fading with blindness, whose ears are dimming so you have to speak very loudly to her. I don't think you can know her and not walk away saying, "What's she got, and how do I get it? What does she know, and where did she learn it?" It seems to be the dividend of seventy-five years or ninety-five years of letting God love you.

We learned today in the word of God that Wisdom is talking to us; and Wisdom is one of the faces of God. And Wisdom is saying, "I created you. I am the creativity and the imagination that made the world beautiful with every flower and the seas and the mountains. I'm the one who gave you imagination. I'm the one who leads you to joy. And I, Wisdom, look at you and I take delight, I take delight in you."

But the fact is, somewhere along the line, many, many,

many of us learned this kind of demented way of loving. We call it love; I don't think it is love, really. But, it's sort of our human effort at love. It looks a little bit like this: our parents teach us, and I see it all the time. In the neighborhood, I see it with parents; in the parish here, with your little ones. How you parent your kid is so significant! If you spoil your kid rotten, let them know that there are no limits, that's one way to parent. Behind your back, we call those children brats.

But the other way to parent, and the other extreme, is to shame your kid. "You stupid little blah, blah, blah, blah, blah." By the time they're five years old, they have this sense that they're kinda stupid, that they're dumb, and they learn they're not wonderful at all.

Or we look at our culture and our culture tells us we all need to have perfect bodies. Our culture out there says that to be happy, you got to tattoo yourself up these days. You gotta pierce this, that, and the other thing. Let your imagination go anywhere it wants. You gotta own this; you gotta drive a Beemer. You need to have a Mercedes. You gotta have a boat. You gotta have a jet ski. You gotta have two or three residences. Cuz that's achieving the dream; that's the American way. More is better.

So many of us chasing, chasing after some toy, some thing, some event, something to make us happy. Something to tell us we're in a world that's loving. And all the while, all the while, it's sitting inside us waiting to grow inside us. ...

Something in us holds God back. Often, often, we're consumed with our work. We're consumed with our toys. We're consumed with our finances. We're consumed about our weight and how we look. A thousand preoccupations. Or we're riveted sometimes on the next cigarette. Let's get this Mass over, I gotta have a smoke. Isn't it 5:00 o'clock? I need my drink. A thousand things to preoccupy us. A thousand things to make us happy. And yet, many, many, many of us in our culture are not happy.

We're looking for the right relationship, that perfect other person to make me happy. When all along, the love of God is enough. When all along, God has been sayin: Jack, I knew you in your mother's womb, I have always loved you. I know your secrets. I know your history. I know your dreams. I know your hopes. I know what's been good about your marriage. I know what's been bad about your marriage. I know all about you. And I absolutely love you. Will you let me love you? Will you let me into your heart? Will you let your spirit be filled up with the great 'aha' that I am loved?

When I look at Sister Mary Regina, I think one of the things we love about her is that she knows she's loved. She walks and lives out of this posture, very daily, Monday, Tuesday, Wednesday, Thursday. Life in the monastery there isn't overly exciting, I bet. You know? And yet living in this awesome awareness that she is loved. That is Wisdom. That is Wisdom. To look in the mirror and say, "I am so loved, so filled up, so blessed, that I must be loved and I must pour myself out, and I must become a blessing to others."

We have this notion in our culture and in our society that if I give a lot of my time away, I'm not going to have any time left for me. Or if I give my money away, I'm not going to have enough for me, or if I give my heart away, my heart is going to go empty. And the reality is quite the opposite. The paradox of Wisdom says: When I empty myself, I can't really get empty because the love of God is pouring into me, and pouring into me and pouring into me, always filling me up.

And that's what the Trinity is.

The Trinity, and I could talk in all kinds of other

terminology, or I could read you some great things from Beatrice Beauteau, that I was reviewing yesterday. But this is what the Trinity is: It is the first community that ever was. It is this intimate community where love meets love; and they meet 100% to 100%. Where the Father says, "I love loving you," to the Son, and, "My joy is in giving myself to you, and pouring myself out to you, and in pouring myself out to my Son, I am filled up." And the Son says to the Father, "I love loving you, and when I pour myself into you, I am filled up, and I am joyful, and we are complete." And this is the way it works.

It's not like half of our marriages, and half of our love relationships, where you say, "I gave a lot more than you gave this week." And "I sent you five cards in the last six months; have I gotten one lousy card from you? I send you flowers; what do I get from you?" rě, rě, rě, rě, rě, and these relationships that we manage to fight our way through, (and how's the marriage?)

What happens when we start loving like the Trinity? Loving unconditionally, not, I'll love you if you do this. But, I love you. I just love you. And loving with measurement: I gave a little more, you gave a little more. But loving without measure.

Just the joy of giving my heart to you. And the joy of letting you give your heart to me. But even if you don't give your heart to me, Melissa, God is loving me enough to give my heart to you anyway. That's the way God is. What a concept. What a concept.

I want to point to two people in our congregation. They had their 45th anniversary vows yesterday: Jerry Steffens and Judy. They've become good friends of mine. When I met Jerry the first day here, when I was kind of checkin' the place out with Julie, the secretary, to see if just maybe I might kinda' sorta' think of maybe comin' to the north side here, in he walks and he says "Hi, I'm Jerry Steffens, and this is my son, we're fixin' the air conditioning today." And I had no idea what he was like. But I can say this: In the last almost four years that I have been here, I have seen him at this plant hundreds of times, fixin' whatever needs to be fixed, finding nothing too small, too menial, too beneath him, giving endless hours of his expertise, and always happy to do it. Not sayin', I put a lot more time in here than Jan Kormann does. I put a lot more time in here than so and so does. Never.

And when he's doin' it he loves to chat. And we talk about life. And right now, he has some cancer he's dealin' with and I've got my stuff I'm dealin' with. And we talked about the fact that everyday is gift. And everyday is love's opportunity. It's just such a gift to be alive.

And then I look at their marriage, which we renewed yesterday. These two people really love each other. I have never heard either of them speak an ill word about each other. I know they've had their fights. I know they've had their struggles. They know they've had their struggles. I have never heard them speak ill of each other. I have heard them delight in their children and whatever their children's needs have been. She takes him to all his treatments for cancer. Wants to be there, wants to love him, right to the end, wherever that goes, whatever it involves, because love meets love meets love and therein is God.

This morning, the gift of God, the most precious thing that is wrapped around us whether we know it or not, is waiting to be received more in this minute than in a minute ago. Take a moment; close your eyes; say "yes" to that gift. Let yourself be filled with the love of the Trinity. And then be unafraid to love, unafraid to serve, unafraid to die … because the love within us has always been enough. The love within us has always been enough.

Chapter 2

I I th Sunday of Ordinary Time, June 17, 2001

Corpus Christi

Similarly here, every person is needed. This church does not exist to offer kinda' funky and nice worship with jazz songs, so people can go back and dismiss the experience. This is simply what we do on Sunday to remember who we are on Monday, Tuesday, Wednesday, Thursday, Friday. This is what we do to be changed and to remember our name and our identity.

- Father Greg Tolaas

Gospel

Luke 7: 11-17

[11] Soon afterward Jesus went to a town named Nain, accompanied by his disciples and a large crowd. [12] Just as he arrived at the gate of the town, a funeral procession was coming out. The dead man was the only son of a woman who was a widow, and a large crowd from the town was with her. [13] When the Lord saw her, his heart was filled with pity for her, and he said to her, "Don't cry." [14] Then he walked over and touched the coffin, and the men carrying it stopped. Jesus said, "Young man! Get up, I tell you!" [15] The dead man sat up and began to talk, and Jesus gave him back to his

mother.

[16] They all were filled with fear and praised God. "A great prophet has appeared among us!" they said; "God has come to save his people!"

[17] This news about Jesus went out through all the country and the surrounding territory.

Homily

Every once in a while, when you're the pastor of a place, you are so close to what's going on that you lose perspective. You lose clarity. Some days you're encouraged, and you don't even know why, and some days you're discouraged, and you can't name quite why. But you're just this close, closer than your nose to the whole of the experience. And once in a while, it's great to hear others assess what's goin' on.

You as congregation should hear what your parish council has assessed about what is going on. We had our sort of year-end review and these are some of the things brought up. Now we have a member of the council who is eighty years old. We have long-time parishioners on the council. We have some new folks, some young folks. We have people of color. We have white folks. It's a mix of us, like a mix of us on Sunday. This is what people said.

We have moving and prayerful worship. Joyful worship. We have increased involvement of parishioners. We have a vibrant prayer chain; what a good idea this year, to start that.

We have a beautiful peace garden. Neighbors and parishioners, kids all over the place, usin' it all the time.

We have hired Hilary, it's kinda' like Cher or Madonna; Hilary doesn't even need a last name. She's just Hilary. To work as a community organizer in this neighborhood. She does great things and helps us and neighbors do great things.

The 10:00 o'clock Mass time has been a good thing, even though it was painful for us. Praying over our sick by all of us laying hands on them; that's a cool thing, somebody thought. The recent practice we have of burning cds and sending them to our shut-ins in the nursing home, so they can listen to the Mass and the marvelous homilies that they would otherwise miss. [laughter]

Good stuff in the bulletin, that we have a strong outer life beyond these walls. We are involved in relationship with our neighbors. That we are of one mind and one heart. Lots of parishes aren't. Lots of parishes are just divided and split and encamped in their various ideologies, heels dug in. We are not.

Journey of Faith, Wednesday nights, twelve sessions we had this past year; got rave reviews. One night we had over 105 people who came for adult enrichment there. Many nights, sixty and seventy.

We have radical hospitality. We have an ongoing invitation to our neighbors, and we don't get discouraged. We just keep inviting. That's a good thing.

Summer concerts, the Patchwork Quilt programs, Kids' Club, College Bound, Teen Endeavor, Compassionate Companion, Women of Great Hope and Vision, Men About Change, which is a very new initiative for men in our neighborhood. These are important; glad we're doin' it.

The new hoops, right out here. The other night I came up from a meeting, where we were looking at next year's Journey of Faith, and making choices, and I counted fifty-eight young people playin' ball in that parking lot. Called 'em all together, stopped everybody, lots of young men who were eighteen, nineteen, twenty, twenty-one, twenty-three, twenty-five years old, their girlfriends there, etc., etc., pulled everybody together. Kids from four years old on.

Talked to 'em for two minutes. Welcome. Love havin' you here. Use this place. Also, come pray with us. Three rules: No vulgarity; No violence or drugs; and No litter. We don't want to litter this little campus of ours. Cuz the banners are beautiful; the garden is beautiful; we are beautiful; and it is time to treat this neighborhood as if it is beautiful. Everybody says, "Right on, thumbs up, let's play ball." I came back that night. No litter.

We are truly a family of faith! We have great music here!

The Compassionate Companion program which for those of you who don't know about it, it is one adult matched up with one child or one teenager in this neighborhood for one year. To love them and believe in that kid, and to let that kid love you and believe in you, that's equally important. The fact that we have wonderful kids by the dozens and dozens and dozens and dozens is very important.

What were the negatives? What do we need to work on? There are things we need to work on. But it had a theme. It was interesting. That we need more hospitality even. More on Saturdays at Mass. Better communication about what's going on. Draw upon more people. Perhaps create a website. Webpage, excuse me. Use the Northsider paper more often for P.R., etc. and continue to reach out to people, especially our sisters and brothers in the church who feel alienated. Sometimes we call them lapsed Catholics.

I need to say that the past two weeks have enriched me because I have believed in a couple of moments down into my guts and my toes that St. Philip is simply this: alive and loving. And unfortunately, there are so many churches about which you cannot say they are alive or loving. What happens to us and what happened to us that we've kind of gotten into over the centuries, this mindset that I have a very privatized relationship with Him, and that in that privatized relationship, I go to church, I do my duty, and then I leave with no consciousness that I am connected to the other people in that building. And NO consciousness that people beyond that building belong to me and I belong to them. That's sort of to me a model of church at its worst. What we decline to do at times, this very privatized thing. I come for communion; I get the sacred cookie and I leave. But I'm not moved to reach out beyond myself. I'm not moved to grow in relationship with the broader world. I'm not moved to serve other people. Yuchchch! I'm busy!

And yet, at St. Philip, there is, and you can feel it; many of you feel it; many of you talk about it. There is this kind of contagious thing that has taken off. It's not about Fr. Greg, cuz if it had been, when we did our review the other night, somebody would have said, "Well one of the good things about St. Philip is Fr. Greg"! [laughter]) But Nooo [more laughter]). Little did I know that I should have slipped somebody a ten to make it to the bottom of the chart. But do you know what the exciting thing is? The exciting thing is this: parishioners have stopped saying, "your garden, your program, your kids, your that". It isn't my garden. It isn't my church. It isn't my programs. It isn't about me. It is about us. That's what the Body of Christ means.

You know, I've had some kidney issues lately, and I've got fingernails that are really thin and they're crackin' and splittin', and it feels like your life is falling apart when your fingernails aren't quite right. And normally you don't think about your nails much. They don't seem real important. But from the smallest piece of the body to the core organs of the body, to the gift of sight and the senses that we enjoy, every piece of the body is important. Every piece is important. Right down to fingernails and toenails and we miss 'em when they're not workin' right.

Similarly here, every person is needed. This church does not exist to offer kinda' funky and nice worship with jazz songs, so people can go back and dismiss the experience. This is simply what we do on Sunday to remember who we are on Monday, Tuesday, Wednesday, Thursday, Friday. This is what we do to be changed and to remember our name and our identity.

I want to pick on, for just a second, Adam and Meghan, another couple in the parish. To be very honest with you, I met Adam through very strange circumstances. I was in Israel studying years ago. This guy says, "I have this friend Adam. Adam is an actor and a singer and he works in New York in theater, and blah, blah, blah, blah, blah."

Then I'm back at the University of St. Thomas, doin' my thing. One Sunday this Adam comes up to me. He goes, "Hi. I'm Adam. My friend is David Chinquebrinady from New York. You were in Israel with him." Wow! "I've moved to St. Paul and I'm going to be working here."

So time goes on and I see Adam in church quite often. And then I come to St. Philip and I see Adam at church. And then he says: "I'm marrying this beautiful young woman."

And I met her; she seemed very nice, but didn't seem at all religious. And she didn't seem like she'd be all that much into church, and I guess she wasn't all that much into church.

But curiously, in their very young marriage, she came. Was it Christmas or something? Okay, Mother's Day? Mother's Day. And something touched her in this room.

And she said, "This is a right place. This is a good place. This is a place I'm comin' back to next Sunday. And the next Sunday. And the next Sunday. And the next Sunday, and the next Sunday." And they have worshiped together most of the Sundays. And when he isn't there for some reason, she still comes. And as touching as this is, the two of them, young as their marriage is, have decided to offer weekend respite care for children who are in crisis. Weekend after weekend, you will see them here with a different baby in their arms. Beautiful children, black children, white children, it doesn't matter. They take this child, have it for a short time, love it to death, and then hand it back, which is hard to do, I'm sure, sometimes, knowing that some day they will have children of their own. But what moves people to make that choice? What moves people, instead of [on] Friday nights, saying, "My God, get me my Manhattan," and "My time is for me, now, on the weekend."

And I feel that. We all feel that. What moves people to say, "Let's go pick up this stranger baby that we're going to have for the weekend and by the end of the weekend, the baby will not be a stranger. And let's love that baby all weekend, change its dirty diapers, hold it, cuddle it, kiss it, pray over it." That's what it means to be a Eucharistic Christian.

And their marriage is so much more alive, and so much bigger, and so much more joyful and so much more deep than if I'm Adam and I'm into Meghan, and I'm Meghan and I'm into Adam, and we're just into us. And we don't go to church; and we just have cappuccino on Sunday morning and we read the paper [while] overlooking Loring Park.

There's a lot of people doin' that this weekend. A lot of people. We have come here to be fed. It says in the Gospel, in that chapter 9, just before the reading we heard, Jesus chose twelve. Then he said to them, "You go out." He sent 'em out right away. "You go out. I give you full authority to expel demons, and to heal." They went out. They came back reporting the marvelous things they had done. They couldn't believe what they were able to do.

Then we get to this reading, which is the next reading. All these people gathered. They had not invited them. They had gone off to Bethsaida, a secluded place, but people followed them. And they gathered and gathered and gathered in great numbers. Thousands of men, not even bothering to count the women or children. So, triple the number or quadruple the number gathered there, and Jesus looks, and it says that Jesus welcomed them. That's what two translations say: "He welcomed them."

And then the disciples say and the apostles say, "Tell them to go. This is more than we can handle. Tell them to leave."

Jesus says, "You feed them."

"We feed them? How are we going to feed them? How are we twelve going to feed them?"

How are we, a small parish in North Minneapolis, going to feed others? How are we going to be bread for them? How are we going to be Christ for them? We can't do it. We don't have the resources. We don't have enough people. Bull!

If the Spirit exists, and the Spirit does, and if there's love in the world, and there still is, the Gospel makes sense, and yes it does. And if Jesus is alive, in the glory of the Father, and he is, then we find our best joy in making a difference. We don't come here just to do our Sunday fix. We come here to be fed and to remember how to be a body, and how to include others in our body.

Two years from now, we better have two Sunday Masses on Sunday morning, with a full church. If we don't, it will be because we have not been hospitable enough. We have not invited others. We have not made them feel welcome. And we have not helped them catch the Spirit of God.

There is a great work to do. We have all that we need to do it. We're already doin' it. Beautifully. But two years from now, we should have a full church, twice on Sunday morning, at least. Full of color, full of young and old, full of people from all over the place, people who find this church community safe.

I look out this morning. I see members of the gay community or the lesbian community. This morning in this room. In all of the fear, in all of the secrecy that people have lived with, so much of their lives, and I say to myself, "This ought to be a room and this ought to be a crowd where our love is so much bigger than our fear and our hatred and our prejudice, because we are ignited by the Spirit."

One final sentence: When you come forward this morning, please, be intentional, be grateful, and remember, it is one bread, one cup, one Lord, one Faith. We are one.

Chapter 3

12th Sunday of Ordinary Time, June 24, 2001

But, I've come to believe, that when we enter into relationship with one another, when you know my story and I know your story, when we sit at the same table, and share a meal, when one of us actually invites a neighbor to come to church, meets them at the door and walks them up the street, that changes the world. That creates relationship. And we bump into each other, and we bump into each other's dreams and stories, and humor and spirituality and goodness and struggle. And all of us are changed.

- Father Greg Tolaas

Gospel Reading

Luke 9: 18-24

18 One day when Jesus was praying alone, the disciples came to him. "Who do the crowds say I am?" he asked them.

19 "Some say that you are John the Baptist," they answered. "Others say that you are Elijah, while others say that one of the prophets of long ago has come back to life."

20 "What about you?" he asked them. "Who do you say I am?"

Peter answered, "You are God's Messiah."

[21] Then Jesus gave them strict orders not to tell this to anyone. [22] He also told them, "The Son of Man must suffer much and be rejected by the elders, the chief priests, and the teachers of the Law. He will be put to death, but three days later he will be raised to life."

[23] And he said to them all, "If you want to come with me, you must forget yourself, take up your cross every day, and follow me. [24] For if you want to save your own life, you will lose it, but if you lose your life for my sake, you will save it."

Homily

There is a saying I heard in the past year that struck my ear strangely. It said, "The rich oppress the poor, and the poor oppress the poor." The rich oppress the poor, and the poor, whom do they oppress? The poor.

You may recall a couple of years ago, three years ago, when the Clinton/Lewinsky scandal was taking place, I talked one day about an editorial I read in a magazine. I think it was Newsweek. People in Russia reported they really did not care if their leaders were immoral personally. They expect their leaders to be immoral personally. They expect their leaders to be corrupt. What makes a good leader in Russia is not if you have moral ethics and if you are uncorrupt. What makes a good leader is if you give the people sausage. If they have abundance and enough to eat, then you are a good leader. And if they do not have enough to eat, then you are a bad leader. And, quite honestly, it reported that people don't necessarily care if their neighbor doesn't have sausage. The president is good if I have sausage.

What do we think about poverty? Ugly an animal it is. But do we think about it at all? Oftentimes our whole sense of poverty is that poverty, if it is not mine, doesn't exist. If it isn't in my neighborhood, it isn't a reality.

And oftentimes, we might say, "I pray for the poor." But I think sometimes the prayer is like this: God bless and keep the poor – far away from me. God bless and keep the poor – out of my neighborhood.

That is often our prayer. Our choice is to isolate ourselves from the poor, and to make sure that they are not in our world, and we are not in their world. And then the world is okay, cuz I've got sausage!

What does poverty spawn? I've been studying it for about four years, day in and day out. Poverty spawns illiteracy, depression, lethargy. Poverty spawns malnutrition in children, and in adults: dependency, laziness. It spawns self-abuse and abuse of others, lots of domestic violence. Poverty spawns low self-esteem, a lack of a dream. It spawns hopelessness, anger, apathy, chemical dependency up the ying-yang, violence in the streets, and in the house, self-hatred, rage, and despair. That is the fruit of poverty.

So who of us, in this room, hate poverty? Who of us actually feel some passion and hatred for it? Oh yeah, not just, poverty is a bummer. Yeah, there's some poverty up there on the Northside. There's some poverty over there in Frogtown. There's some poverty over in the Southside, by Lake Street there. Hmmm. Bummer. Turn the page.

Who of us has ever been filled with a passion to hate poverty and what it does to destroy the soul, and destroy our creativity? And destroy imagination? The saddest thing for me is that by the time many children in our neighborhood are twelve years old, they've got no passion. They're not dreamin' dreams about their future. They're being invited to hustle dope by somebody six years older than they are.

Go down 26th Street. You can stop at about five corners before you ever get to St. Anne's, with teenagers and young men sellin' dope and on the hustle. I was down lookin' in

Merwin's parking lot, watchin' a deal the other day, by the red light, waitin' to take my left. It's pathetic.

In walk the Prophets.

This morning we heard from Isaiah. This morning we hear about the birth of John. This morning we listen to the Gospel of Jesus. Isaiah, John and Jesus, three prophetic voices. Three voices that loathed and hated poverty. And more than just hating poverty, Isaiah, John and Jesus were people who entered into the world of the poor. Who walked with the poor, ate with the poor, encouraged the poor. And also challenged those who oppressed the poor.

Now, I have no need to romanticize poverty and say, "All the people in Frogtown are beautiful. And all the people on Lake Street are beautiful. And all the people on the Northside, who are living in poverty, are beautiful." They are beautiful, in the sense that they are God's children. But many of them do not know they are God's children. Many of them learn to be vicious, just trying to survive.

There is such a need for people to live prophetic lives. And what do I mean by that?   One thing I mean by that is this: to step out of your comfort zone enough to learn to know and love one person or one family who lives in poverty.

Because if you get to know them, if you get to care about them, if you get to believe in them, if you get to love them, you will be changed and they will be changed. But as long as we stay in separate worlds, and say a little prayer once in a while that poverty will end, that will not change it, will it? It hasn't changed it for twenty centuries, since Jesus was here. The poor are still poor and there are many.

But, I've come to believe, that when we enter into relationship with one another, when you know my story and I know your story, when we sit at the same table, and share a meal, when one of us actually invites a neighbor to come to church, meets them at the door and walks them up the street, that changes the world. That creates relationship. And we bump into each other, and we bump into each other's dreams and stories, and humor and spirituality and goodness and struggle. And all of us are changed.

Who are the ones who keep the poor, poor? You know who keeps the poor, poor? The dealers of drugs, both the big drug lords and the small on-the-street dealers. They're keepin' the poor, poor.

Those who create welfare systems, but never enter into the lives of the poor and create dependency - that keeps the poor, poor.

Fathers who abandon the responsibility to raise their children, cuz they're clueless that they really have that privilege and responsibility. They are keeping their children poor.

People who make millions of dollars or plenty of money, let's just put that away, and hoard it, just giving a tiny bit of the icing on the cake away when absolutely necessary, they're keepin' the poor, poor.

Governments who supply shabby schools and programs that don't work are keepin' the poor, poor.

Parents and citizens, that's us, who allow children to grow up in violence, and extreme need, we are keepin' the poor, poor.

Liquor stores at the end of this street, down here, Lyndale and Broadway, sellin' tons of malt liquor, unconditionally, to anybody who wants to drink 'til they're out of their mind on Saturday night. That's keepin' the poor, poor.

Companies who underpay and anyone who isolates themselves from the poor - we are keepin' the poor, poor.

The fact is, after awhile it is amazing and dismaying to

me, and I believe to God, to look at what becomes of the poor. There is great apathy. There is great hopelessness. I go up and down this street on Sunday mornings, door-to-door, inviting people to come and pray and very, very, very few do it. So deep is the depression, so deep is the whatever it is. What if fifty of us reached out, knew their names, invited them? "I'll meet cha. We'll come to church together." Might it be a little different?

Many of you, not all, but many of you, are reaching beyond yourselves, to know at least one person who lives in struggle and economic poverty. Many of you are willing to spend some time with them. But it's amazing what happens to us.

How many of us say, "I have no time for that". Or, "The poor, they're not my thing. Sorry." Or "I'm gonna' get around to it but I've really been kinda' busy."

There are so many reasons not to leave our comfort zone. But there are always more reasons to leave our comfort zone. One of them is love. And the invitation to live a life that matters; live a life that is prophetic.

Three names: Isaiah, John the Baptist, Jesus; all were anointed; all were called; all were prophetic; all were full of passion; all of them full of love. They came to tell the truth. To live the truth. To walk with those who were hurting. And to change the world.

That is our call. Isaiah, very called. John, very called. Jesus, very called. Amidst my own struggle to respond, and my own failure to respond at times, I believe I, too, have been given the exact same call. And what about you? To what are you called? To what will you answer?

Chapter 4

13th Sunday of Ordinary Time, July 1, 2001

This is the moment. This is the time. This is the gift. This is the love. It is offered right now. Don't turn back. Don't look back. Turn your face to the light. Turn your face to the name, Jesus.

- Father Greg Tolaas

Gospel Reading

Luke 9:51-62

⁵¹ As the time drew near when Jesus would be taken up to heaven, he made up his mind and set out on his way to Jerusalem. ⁵² He sent messengers ahead of him, who went into a village in Samaria to get everything ready for him. ⁵³ But the people there would not receive him, because it was clear that he was on his way to Jerusalem. ⁵⁴ When the disciples James and John saw this, they said, "Lord, do you want us to call fire down from heaven to destroy them?"

⁵⁵ Jesus turned and rebuked them. ⁵⁶ Then Jesus and

his disciples went on to another village.

⁵⁷ As they went on their way, a man said to Jesus, "I will follow you wherever you go."

⁵⁸ Jesus said to him, "Foxes have holes, and birds have nests, but the Son of Man has no place to lie down and rest."

⁵⁹ He said to another man, "Follow me."

But that man said, "Sir, first let me go back and bury my father."

⁶⁰ Jesus answered, "Let the dead bury their own dead. You go and proclaim the Kingdom of God."

⁶¹ Someone else said, "I will follow you, sir; but first let me go and say goodbye to my family."

⁶² Jesus said to him, "Anyone who starts to plow and then keeps looking back is of no use for the Kingdom of God."

Homily

Before I offer a few words of reflection this morning, I'm gonna ask you to either close your eyes, or, to fix your eyes upon the crucifix on the wall. And I'm gonna ask you to slowly, with each breath, simply say the name, "Jesus." Kinda the first part of His name on the inhalation, "sus" on the exhalation. "Jesus." Ten breaths, ten times. Center your heart. Breathe deep enough to let His spirit breathe deep into you. <Jesus> <Jesus> <Jesus> <Jesus> <Jesus> Let go of other thoughts and distractions and preoccupations. Simply say His name over and over. <Jesus> <Jesus> <Jesus> <Jesus> <Jesus> <Jesus> <Jesus> <Jesus> <Jesus> <Jesus>.

Now, come back to me, if you would.

This past week I was in Rochester, Minnesota, with the priests of our Archdiocese; we are about 350. We gathered with our auxiliary bishops and our bishop, Harry Flynn. And oftentimes, in these gatherings, it is pretty typical of us, for the Conservatives to find the Conservatives, and the ultra Conservatives to find the ultra Conservatives, and the Liberals to find the Liberals, and the Centrists to kinda just "hang out" together in the center and the ultra Liberals with the ultra Liberals. We just love to hang out with the people who are just like us and we talk about the people who aren't like us.

A few years ago, our bishop said to us. "We can do better than this. We must set aside all acrimony. We must set aside all of this temptation to hang out with people who are just like me. And recognize the presence of Christ in one another."

And in the last two assemblies, there has been a different kind of camaraderie, a different kind of fraternity in Christ, a different kind of gentleness, a different kind of honesty, a different kind of joy. I have really loved both of the last two assemblies when we have gathered, because our love has been big, our pettiness small.

And at the end of this week, on Thursday, when Archbishop Flynn got up to speak, he did what he kind of always does to us. He called us simply back to Jesus. He said, "The person of Jesus is what it is all about, and experiencing the presence and person of Jesus in each other. That's all that it's about. Everything else comes second to that. Everything else is less in importance for the Christian person."

And I really love to listen to him when he's talking about that because I know that he believes it. I believe him. And I walk away from those assemblies recognizing that he loves the name of Jesus; he loves the person of Jesus, he loves to have relationship with Jesus, and it makes me want to deepen my love for Jesus. It makes me want to deepen my walk with Jesus. That it isn't just about doin' church. It isn't just about sayin' prayers. It isn't just about goin' through the beads. It isn't me sayin' "Oh my God, I never pray, I hate myself." It's about letting this love relationship exist. And letting this love relationship shape our lives.

And so I left Rochester, really stirred up inside and in love with Jesus. And I'm not talking about knowing about Jesus. We all know about Jesus. We hear the priest yammer, yammer, yammer, yammer, and we can read in the Bible stories about Jesus. I'm talkin' about goin' the next step deeper where we let his love pierce our heart, pierce our time, pierce our choices, pierce and bless our relationships. Where we let his love go to work with us. Where we let his love into bed with us. Where we let his love be enough for us.

I want you to think for a moment: who in this room, this past week - don't raise your hands - who in this room this past week said, "Jesus, I receive Your love today, and I love You with all of my heart"? Who of us this week, even once in our consciousness said, Jesus, I love You with all my heart, because You love me with all of your heart. Jesus, be with me in my workday. Jesus, be with me when I sit to eat. Jesus, be with me in the car. Jesus, be with me when I'm facing depression. Jesus, be with me in my marriage or in my courtship and dating. Be with me in my parenting. Be with me as a student. Be with me when I'm sick. Be with me when I'm lonely. Be with me when I'm longing for intimacy and I wonder where I'm gonna get it. Be with me in my sexual life. Be with me in my quiet time. Be with me when I'm traveling. Be with me when I sleep"?

Or, who of us is willing to say, "Jesus, I turn to You and

I want You to teach me. I want You to teach n
I'm lost, when I'm frightened, when I'm angry, when I'm
rageful. I want You to teach me how to react when I have
been hurt, or sinned against, or betrayed. I want You to
teach me to be more honest and less dishonest. I want
You to teach me when I'm overwhelmed and when I'm
scared?"

Or, "Jesus, walk with me, and heal me when I have been
lazy, apathetic, full of prejudice. Be with me when I'm
judgmental. When I offend others. Be with me when I'm
full of myself?"

There is no situation in which the love of Jesus is not the
force we long for. Everybody in this church is looking
for meaning. Everybody in this church is looking for
happiness. Everybody in this church is looking to feel
rooted in their lives. Everybody in this church wants to
belong to somebody.

And we have this incredible God with this incredible
Son, who says, "I am so committed to you, I am so crazy
about you, I am so in love with you, and I have what you
need! You're not gonna find it in any kind of addiction:
addiction to money, addiction to toys, addiction to sex,
addiction to booze, addiction to drugs. You're not gonna

find it anywhere but in this simple gift, that is so available to you. My love is enough. My name is Jesus. Grow into my name. Grow into my Spirit. Grow into the love of the Eucharist."

Why is it that so many people, even in our wonderful congregation, still kind of hem and haw, "Oh, am I gonna go to church this week? I dunno."

Fact is, if you are full of the spirit of Jesus, you don't ask yourself, "am I goin' to church?"

Of course, I'm going to worship. Of course, my presence makes a difference in the assembly. Of course, I want to be fed on the word of God. I want to be fed on the bread of Jesus. I want to be filled up.

If you're hittin' the wall this week, you need the Eucharist. If you're full of gratitude this week, you still need the Eucharist. If you feel in love and happy, you need the Eucharist. And if you're depressed and all alone, you need the Eucharist. We need each other. Jesus in the bread. Jesus in the crowd. Jesus in these words. Jesus in the air. Jesus in the stars. Jesus in the Peace Garden. Jesus on the streets.

I have been hit with a special sadness in the last couple days, cuz with the heat of summer you just see tons and tons of people out on the street. And it's not seeing people that I mind. It's sometimes looking at provocative, provocative outfits, completely sexualized, on the bodies of young women. Why? Why?

We were drivin' home last night and there were three guys, and I remember their faces, when they saw me, Mr. White Man, at Lyndale and Broadway, comin' up Lyndale, there, tryin' to stop me to sell me drugs. Why?

What have we descended to in our culture? That people are so mired in the depression of their lives, so mired in the fruit of poverty, so mired in the culture of drugs, so mired in the sexualness, that some poor girl is goin' to be a mother at sixteen years old. Because somehow we have established, and we have let it go on in our culture, that that's the answer.

THAT AIN'T THE ANSWER! Love is the answer. Relationships are the answer. Jesus is the answer. Eucharist is the answer. The love of Jesus is enough. But who's speaking the love of Jesus to them? And I'm not talkin' about bible-bangin' em over the head. I'm talkin' about who's gonna step out of the comfort zone to speak the name of Jesus to people? And I know the answers, cuz I have the same answers: Cuz I'm too busy. I have so much on my schedule, etc. And oftentimes, I think we don't do it because we're not necessarily allowing ourselves to be full of Jesus.

Were we full of Him, were we full of His love, were we recognizing that deep in our gut, the peace that He brings all of us, myself very included, we would be living our lives, perhaps, differently.

The Scriptures said today that Jesus turned his face toward Jerusalem. He knew what God had asked Him to do. And in love, He did it. We turn our face to Jesus. And we follow Him where He goes.

That Gospel reading was full of examples:

"Lord I'd love to follow You, but I've gotta take care of some business right now."

"Lord I'd love to follow You, but I've gotta say goodbye to my parents."

"Lord, I'd love to follow You, but I've gotta bury the dead."

"Lord, I've got so much to do, I'm gonna follow You tomorrow"!

And Jesus said: You do that tomorrow gig, you'll do it all your life.

This is the moment. This is the time. This is the gift. This is the love. It is offered right now. Don't turn back. Don't look back. Turn your face to the light. Turn your face to the name, Jesus.

I'm gonna invite us to take a few minutes of quiet again. All I ask is that you place that name in your heart. The name of Jesus eventually dispels all fear, it dispels all judgmentalism, it pierces all apathy. It kills hatred. It gives us love.

Let's give ourselves the gift ten more times to say and love that name.   <Jesus> <Jesus> <Jesus> <Jesus> <Jesus> < Jesus > <Jesus> <Jesus> <Jesus> <Jesus>

Chapter 5

15th Sunday of Ordinary Time, July 15, 2001

You and I will have at least 100 opportunities to be loving, or unloving; to be generous, or ungenerous; to be kind, or to be cold. I'm gonna' ask you, embrace the heart of Jesus. Give way to kindness.

- Father Greg Tolaas

Gospel Reading

Luke 10: 25-37

²⁵ A teacher of the Law came up and tried to trap Jesus. "Teacher," he asked, "what must I do to receive eternal life?"

²⁶ Jesus answered him, "What do the Scriptures say? How do you interpret them?"

²⁷ The man answered, "'Love the Lord your God with all your heart, with all your soul, with all your strength, and with all your mind'; and 'Love your neighbor as you love yourself.'"

²⁸ "You are right," Jesus replied; "do this and you will live."

²⁹ But the teacher of the Law wanted to justify himself, so he asked Jesus, "Who is my neighbor?"

³⁰ Jesus answered, "There was once a man who was going down from Jerusalem to Jericho when robbers attacked him, stripped him, and beat him up, leaving him half dead. ³¹ It so happened that a priest was going down that road, but when he saw the man he walked on by on the other side. ³² In the same way a Levite also came there, went over and looked at the man, and then walked on by on the other side. ³³ But a Samaritan who was traveling that way came upon the man, and when he saw him, his heart was filled with pity. ³⁴ He went over to him, poured oil and wine on his wounds and bandaged them; then he put the man on his own animal and took him to an inn, where he took care of him. ³⁵ The next day he took out two silver coins and gave them to the innkeeper. 'Take care of him,' he told the innkeeper, 'and when I come back this way, I will pay you whatever else you spend on him.'"

³⁶ And Jesus concluded, "In your opinion, which one of these three acted like a neighbor toward the man

attacked by the robbers?"

37 The teacher of the Law answered, "The one who was kind to him."

Jesus replied, "You go then, and do the same."

Homily

Lord knows there are many kinds of people in the world. There are people who want to come to church and have a very private experience. There are people who want to come to church and have "Hee-Haw" - have a real warm down country kind of experience, where everybody gets real friendly. There are some people who are really heartened and grateful for the opportunity to greet neighbors when we begin our worship and other people who think "Oh God, again? I thought he might skip that this week."

I read your faces. I know who you are. Mhmm. Mhmm

Kindness demands a bit of energy going out from us, doesn't it?

I was in New York last week for about five days. It is not said to be the warmest fuzziest city in the world. People learn at very young ages to kind of mind their own business, pay heed to their own need, do avoid eye contact whenever possible, and keep on the move with fast walk.

Then one morning I was by myself, and I decided I'm going to be friendlier than I've been. I've been just kind of doing that no eye contact thing. I'm going to be friendlier. So I was at the café, and pretty soon the waitress goes, "Whaddayawant?" And I said, "Good Morning." And she goes, "Good morning whaddayawant?" And by the end of the experience, there was kind of some warmth and rapport happening there and I left a nice big tip. She was happy.

But as I walked through the morning, at one point I dropped my Metro card on the ground and someone says, "Hey, sir, you dropped your Metro card," bent down, picked it up, and gave it to me. Just a moment of kindness.

I was standing at the corner of 14th and such and such, by Union Square. They're doing lots of construction; things were a mess, very hard to negotiate. And next to me was a man who was blind, standing there with his white cane. And I didn't want to be in his face or kind of get into his space, or his life, or kind of assume things for him. But when the light changed, the traffic was confusing. I just turned to him and I said, "Sir, the light has turned green." And without a split second, he just reached out his arm and took my elbow. And I walked him across the street. And there was my skin and his skin touching, as we kind of walked across through the gravel and the mess. Got to the other side. I just stopped and he said, "Thank you." And he went on to live the rest of his life, without me.

Throughout the morning, it was interesting to watch people. When you get onto the subway, it was actually an experience that older people, when they came on, younger people got up and let them sit down.

Kindness is an amazing thing. And a world with kindness is an amazing place. And a world without kindness, without bigness of heart is a nasty and difficult place to live. Kindness is great.

I was walking across the Brooklyn Bridge one afternoon. It was beautiful, just a gorgeous afternoon. Lot of people walking on this walking bridge that is over the traffic level. And these three chubby little boys came walking toward me, and they had bright red sweatshirts on; they were African American kids, pretty round, and they're walkin' along and they were darling kids, 6, 7, 8, 9 years old.

And about a hundred feet behind 'em was a couple, coming along, and I stopped the couple and I said, "Are those your kids?"

They say, "Yes."

I said, "They're the three cutest kids I've seen in New York all day." She said, "Why, thank you so much. Which one do you want?" [laughter]

Kindness isn't really costly.

Kindness is a choice. It is a choice. Today, in that very familiar story, we meet this Samaritan character. And while, with all rules and regulations, he should have hated the Jew, who was lying there on the road, because Samaritans and Jews always hate each other. Them's the rules. He decides to reach out to him. This Samaritan chose kindness. This Samaritan chose inconvenience. This Samaritan chose to cost himself some money, some time, some energy, and to walk and to let the guy ride his animal. This Samaritan chose to have a loving heart.

In Colossians, today, it says, "All things were created through Christ." And then it goes on to say, next phrase, "All things were created for Christ."

When I look out over this congregation, today, I can look and I can say, "Brad Von Bank, why do you exist? Why are you here on the face of the earth?"

And the answer for the Christian person, is really quite simple. I exist for Christ. I exist to allow myself to be loved by the mercy of God, the graciousness of God, the bigness of God, the wonder of God. And then I carry the joyful responsibility to share that with others.

I exist on this earth, not to make three million bucks. I exist on this earth, not to be the highest achiever in corporate America or the best lawyer in the courtroom. I exist to be Christ, for whoever needs me and that's not about pickin' out my favorites. And that's not about just hangin' out with people who are just like me. It is about seeing Christ, on the streets, in the grocery line, at the library, in the work place, in the church. It is about choosing kindness.

As you know, we have new hoops in the lot. And that has been a heavily trafficked little area in the last couple of weeks. It is really quite thrilling. Sometimes there's forty young people out there playin' ball: twenty-year-old men, five-year-old kids, parents coming by to watch.

Well, I came home from New York, and I had said to Joe Langel in our parish, (Joe happens to be here this morning.) I said, "Joe, you play basketball. Could you do something with these kids? I don't know how to dribble. I don't know how to shoot. I don't know anything about basketball. Would you, perhaps, do something organized with these kids?"

So, I come in from New York. I look out the kitchen window and I see all these kids, about 28 kids, it was. And [it was] the first night of basketball camp, havin' a great time, learnin' their drills and their skills, and kind of thrilled about it all. They circled up at the end of it, had a little prayer, had some Kool Aid, blah, blah, blah. And I think to myself, that was a choice. That's a choice on Joe's part. Joe could think ten reasons why not to have basketball camp, ten reasons to say, "It's too hot. I'm too busy. These kids are too unruly. I have my career. I golf on Wednesdays. Blah. Blah."

But to say, "I choose to give my heart and my time and my talent to these kids. I choose to value them and honor them and reach out to them, and give them some precious time when it's inconvenient, as well as when it's convenient. That is kindness. That is what we are called to.

If I had to put it a different way, I would say this: Our mission on earth is to have the heart of Jesus.

And you might say, "How can I possibly have the heart of Jesus? I'm old, I'm crazy, I'm busy, I have these issues in my life."

The First Reading gives us a clue. The First Reading says to us today, "You don't need to look out into the skies to find where am I going to get that goodness of God. You don't need to look across the sea to ask it to come to you. It is already in your hearts. It is already in your mouths." Cherish the gift already given. Everyone in this room is totally loved. Everyone in this room is totally anointed. Everyone in this room is totally blessed. Take the gift given, and become a gift for someone else.

Choose it. It is life.

Once again, to have the heart of Jesus is to have the heart of the Samaritan. This particular Samaritan guy, loathed by many, made some choices. He chose to stop. He chose to care. He chose to anoint a half-dying man. He chose to sacrifice. He chose to pay some money to have him cared for. He chose to engage another human being with kindness.

That is our call.

You and I will have at least 100 opportunities to be loving, or unloving; to be generous, or ungenerous; to be kind, or to be cold. I'm gonna' ask you, embrace the heart of Jesus. Give way to kindness.

Kindness is always a good choice.

Chapter 6

21st Sunday of Ordinary Time, August 26, 2001

Jesus' personality must have been something. And I also believe in the kindness that he showed to the poor and the needy and the broken-in-spirit, which was most of that society. He must have been very kind. And he must have been very joyful. And he must have been quite urgent. And he might have even been unforgettable, for some.

- Father Greg Tolaas

Gospel Reading

Luke 13: 22-30

²² Jesus went through towns and villages, teaching the people and making his way toward Jerusalem. ²³ Someone asked him, Sir, will just a few people be saved?"

Jesus answered them, ²⁴ "Do your best to go in through the narrow door; because many people will surely try to go in but will not be able. ²⁵ The master of the house will get up and close the door; then when you stand outside and begin to knock on the door and say, 'Open the door for us, sir!' he will answer you, 'I don't know where you come from!' ²⁶ Then you will answer 'We ate and drank with you; you taught in our town!' ²⁷ But he will say again, 'I don't know where you come from. Get away from me, all you wicked people!' ²⁸ How you will cry and gnash your teeth when you see Abraham, Isaac, and Jacob, and all the prophets in the Kingdom of God, while you are thrown out! ²⁹ People will come from the east and the west, from the north and the south, and sit down at the feast in the Kingdom of God. ³⁰ Then those who are now last will be first, and those who are now first will be last."

Homily

I have had more than a fair share of opportunity to be with people when they are sick and looking at death, when they are dying. And there are unfortunately too many people, who in their dying say, "I woulda, I coulda, I shoulda."

The life lived with woulda, coulda, and shoulda, is a frustrating life. Hold that in mind with today's gospel.

I want you to think for a moment about the friends you dine with, the people you dine with, the dining events that you have. What are the topics that get talked about? We talk about our kids. We talk about work. We talk about our boss. We talk about vacations. We talk about maybe buyin' this or buyin' that. We talk about sports and shopping and sales. And we Minnesotans, we like to talk about goin' to the lake. Sometimes, if it's good friends, we talk about the problems we're havin' with our kids. We might talk about church. What we like about our church. What we don't like about our pastor. Whatever. With your really intimate friends, you might talk about sex. Not so intimate, you talk about computers or somethin'. We talk about how delicious the food is in this restaurant. We'll have to come back. Or the service has been lousy. We're not gonna be here again. We talk about our grandkids. And our investments. And golf. Etc.

How many of us, in the past month, have sat at table with somebody whom we care about and have earnestly talked about the kingdom of God and our part in it?

Think, for a moment, about what it might have been like to dine with Jesus. The Gospels are really full of experiences of dining with this character called Jesus. What might you talk about, if you were dining with him? Would it be about golf and restaurants and the boss? What did he talk about when he was at table with people? And who did he dine with? Scripture says both the rich and the poor. And who was it that liked dining with him? And who finished dining with Jesus and said, "Not going to do that again."

Jesus' personality must have been something. I was reading a theological book recently that talked about his urgency to bring about the kingdom. I believe that Jesus with this amazing broad following that he had at different times in his ministry, that he must have been very charismatic. And I also believe in the kindness that he showed to the poor and the needy, and the broken-in-spirit, which was most of that society. He must have been very kind. And he must have been very joyful. And he must have been quite urgent. And he might have even been unforgettable, for some.

He ate with Pharisees. He ate with prestigious people. He ate and broke the rules with women. He ate with sinners. He ate with societal scum, who you and I might not choose to eat with. And it troubled the wealthy when they were invited to his table. It troubled the wealthy to say, "Are these scum going to be at your table too?"

"Are these sinners going to be at your table?"

"Are these who are less than I am going to be at your table?"

"Are these who are unclean going to be at your table?"

"We don't dine together."

And Jesus said, "But we do. We do."

When we listen to the story today, it is not an easy story. It says that at the end of our lives, we will come to the door, and the door is narrow. And the Master will come to the door, and the Master may say to us, "I don't know you."

And what do we say? "Huh, but you do know us. My goodness, we ate at your table, time and time again. And you ate at our table. And you taught in our streets. And you taught in our church. And you taught in our neighborhood. We know each other."

And He will say to us, "You bet, I sat at your table, and you sat at mine. And did you listen to what I said to you? And did you change because of what I said to you? Did you grow, table event after table event? Did you grow in compassion for the needy, the poor, the sick, the elderly, the outcast? Did you, after table time together, did you live your life with a different kind of generosity? Did you live your life with a different kind of fire, for Justice? Did it bother you when the KKK met at your Capitol? Did you think about it, much less address it? Or did you just shake your head. 'I don't have the time or the energy to be concerned about such things.'"

"And were you full of mercy? I sat at your table. I taught you mercy. I AM Mercy. Did you show mercy to the poor and the needy?"

You and I know that we are in a very unique neighborhood, with unique and blessed opportunities to bump into the invitation to compassion, and justice, and mercy. There are such needs.

This past week I was thinkin' about my life, what I like about it, what I don't. What's gratifying. What's hard. To be honest about this with you, I was thinking about my visits to the sick. How sad those can feel. I thought about watching drug deals go on and the two times this week that drugs were offered to me. I thought about the children who go hungry sometimes, without two meals or three in a day, in our neighborhood. I thought about the lonely woman who, the lovely woman, excuse me, who died of cancer. She came to our church, about five times, Marie's cousin. She had just heard she was full of cancer. She and I had one hour together, in my office, to talk. We talked. We prayed.

She said, "I'm gonna make this. I'm gonna fight this. I'm

gonna beat this. I want to live." She went to chemo on Tuesday, had respiratory failure, cardiac failure. She's dead. She was young. She was beautiful.

I think of the people in my life and in our lives who live with depression, who live with loneliness. I think of the mothers who I know by name, who have their water cut off, whose rent is $1,000 or $1,100 a month, who are raising four and five and seven children. And I never even have to think about them if I don't want to.

I think about the people who came to our door, some with real needs, some just tellin' a story to get some cash.

I think about the illiteracy that abounds in our world. I think about my friend, Ginny Kelly, whose cancer in her body is so painful, that she is bed ridden, with three little girls, watching their mother die.

There is so much to cry about. There is so much sadness. There is so much broken, that we are tempted to turn our face away.

But Jesus says, "When you sit at my table, and when you listen to my teaching, it is all about compassion and justice and mercy. I am compassion. You must be. I am justice.

You must be. I am mercy. You must be mercy."

If we are not these things, I don't care what toys we have, I don't care how fat our portfolio looks, we will not be happy.

At the end of our life, which could happen this week, or next year, or in fifty years, who knows? But at the end of our life, Scripture tells us, Jesus tells us, "You will come to the narrow door. The Master will come to the door. He will either know you, or He won't. You will either have known Him, or you won't." And when we say, "Lord, I ate at your table, You ate at my table. You taught in my church. You taught in our streets." He will say to you and to me, "Yes, I did. And what did you learn? And how did you live? Were you full of compassion? Did you act justly? To whom did you show a kindness or mercy?"

Some of us will enter the door. Praise God. Some may grind teeth, and wail. It doesn't ever have to be that way.

At the end of your life, I hope you are not, and I am not, one of those people who say, geez, "I woulda, I coulda, I shoulda."

Chapter 7

22nd Sunday of Ordinary Time, September 2, 2001

On the other hand, you show me a person who believes God's love is enough. You show me a person who believes they are eternally loved by the Eternal Lover, and most likely, I'll be able to show you somebody very willing to step forward to serve, to give, to love, to share. I'll show you somebody who's free.

- Father Greg Tolaas

Gospel Reading

Luke 14: 1, 7-14

¹ One Sabbath Jesus went to eat a meal at the home of one of the leading Pharisees; and people were watching Jesus closely.

⁷ Jesus noticed how some of the guests were choosing the best places, so he told this parable to all of them: ⁸ "When someone invites you to a wedding feast, do not sit down in the best place. It could happen that someone more important than you has been invited, ⁹ and your host, who invited both of you, would have to come and say to you, 'Let him have this place.' Then

you would be embararssed and have to sit in the lowest place. [10] Instead, when you are invited, go and sit in the lowest place, so that your host will come to you and say, 'Come on up, my friend, to a better place.' This will bring you honor in the presence of all the other guests. [11] For those who make themselves great will be humbled, and those who humble themselves will be made great."

[12] Then Jesus said to his host, "When you give a lunch or a dinner, do not invite your friends or your brothers or your relatives or your rich neighbors - for they will invite you back, and in this way you will be paid for what you did. [13] When you give a feast, invite the poor, the crippled, the lame, and the blind; [14] and you will be blessed, because they are not able to pay you back. God will repay you on the day the good people rise from death."

Homily

Some ideas or insights are very contagious to the soul.

I have a friend who has a friend, and her friend taught her that every time she takes a shower, she decides to relive her Baptism. And so my friend picked up on the idea and she says, "Every time I shower, I relive my Baptism." And I thought, "Wow! What a concept!"

And I tried it on, and it was an amazing experience, to allow, in the washing of that water, to allow God's love to wash over me. And to allow God's grace to cleanse me and to offer me healing and forgiveness. To allow the warmth of that water to remind me of the great mercy that surrounds me. To stand in that shower, that Baptism moment again and again. And let go of my sins. And let go of my grudges. Let go of the crap that poisons my soul. To be surrounded in the wash in love. Wow! What a concept! What a concept. How awesome to live our Baptism consciously, every day!

So, if some morning, when you're coming to Mass, and you're here a little early, if you happen to hear alleluias coming out of the rectory on the backend of the building, you'll know I'm in the shower, doing my God thing in the morning.

When we take time to allow God's love and God's power, and God's peace, and God's graciousness to penetrate our souls, we become different. Think about it for a moment. When you have been in love with somebody, really, really, you love that person so much, and you realize that he/she loves you back so much, don't you feel alive, and you can kind of take on the world, and you can do whatever you have to do. You're full of an inner energy, because of knowing you're loved!

On the other side of that coin, when you feel like nobody loves you, when you feel alienated and alone, you want to stay in bed, curled up, fetal, depressed, powerless, without energy. When a love is good, we feel alive. When a love has gone sour, we feel quite dead. We all want to be loved.

And I stand here today, to say to you, whether or not there is any human person loving you, and the fact is, I believe all of us are loved by particular human beings. And that's a good thing. But even if that was not the case, every person in this room, every person on the face of the earth, is absolutely, eternally, fully, deeply loved by the God whose love is enough for us. By the God whose grace is enough for us. By the God whose mercy is so abundant for us that were we to be in touch with all of that love, we would fall over. We could not contain the joy and the delight of knowing I am fully loved by the author of the universe. I am deeply loved by Jesus, brother, friend, savior. I am deeply awash in the Spirit.

But today's readings don't really seem to be about love. We're told about humility.

I'm gonna ask you a question. Can you be humble and know you are humble? Think about it for a moment. Can you be authentically humble and know that you are humble? I am so humble. [laughter] It doesn't work. It doesn't work. Can you be all fixated on how's my humility lately? I think it's really, really good. To think that way is to be unhumble. Humility is a funny animal. Humility is what happens to us when we allow love to pierce our heart, and pierce our mind, and pierce our behaviors, and change how we are in the world.

When you feel absolutely loved, and when you know you are absolutely loved, you behave differently, you just do! Actually, humility is the unconscious effect of experiencing God's unceasing love for us. When we feel loved, when we know we are loved, when we are free to love, when we are free to receive it, and free to give it, then humility has a chance to grow in us.

When I am drinking in God's love, when I am drinking in the saving love of Jesus, when I am drinking in the power and the presence of the Spirit, I become more gentle, I become more forgiving, I become more tolerant, and more patient. When I'm drinking in the saving love of God, lettin' it wash over me and lettin' it come into me, I become also more generous. More able to share my time, my talents, my efforts. I'm not kind of measuring it. I'm not giving any more time to the church. I'm really busy with my job, and my this and my this and my this. Now back to me. When we know through our being we are loved, we are freer to give. And, when we know we are loved, we also don't feel a need to measure.

We've all been in those relationships, our spousal relationships, our parent-child relationships, our brother-sister relationships. I gave more to you than you gave to me; I'm always attentive to you and you're not attentive to me. By the way, my birthday was yesterday. We measure, measure, measure, measure.

When we are awash in God's love, and that love is enough for us, we don't feel the need to measure all of the time. And we don't need your love or your love or your love to complete us. God's love already completes me. I am already rooted in love, rooted in life, able to love you, whether or not you love me back. Think of it! What it would be like to be that free to love you, even if you don't love me back. That's an awesome power. That's an awesome freedom.

When I am washed in God's immense love, and when I come to the banquet, whatever that banquet is, I don't need to measure. Am I in a place of prestige? Am I in a place where people will notice me? Am I in a place where I feel powerful? We're just so happy to be invited to the banquet, and we're so loved walkin' in the door, that it doesn't matter if we sit at the bottom place or the top place.

And yet, if you are like I am, I have spent plenty of time in my life wondering who's noticing me, who's appreciating me? "Do I have a little prestige here? Do you know who I am?"

And the story of Jesus is saying, when the posture we live in is loved, deeply loved, truly loved, we are happy to sit anywhere at the banquet. We are simply happy to be invited. And God is enough. And that's why that song makes sense: "Lord, Give me your Love and Your Grace. That is enough for me." You can have my time. You can have my work. You can have my money. You can have my sexual longings. You can have all of me. Because when I give all of me to you, I find happy. What a recipe! When I give my Spirit over to that great wash of love, then I am happy. Then, I want to work for justice. Then, I want to share my time and my energy. Then, I am accepting of people who are different than I am. Instead of just gravitating toward my buddies and my friends and the people who are just like me!

Think of all the fears we have that keep us from loving radically. Think of the many of us who never achieve humility. Mostly because we have not believed how loved we are. And we have let fear and comparison and prestige and power and things drive our lives. Only love, only love, should be drawing our architectural plan, only love should drive our lives.

You show me a person who is fixated on himself or herself. You show me a person who is worried about prestige. You show me a person for whom their things and their toys are very important. You show me a person who is always measuring in their relationships, and I'll show you somebody who does not know truly God's love for them and has not allowed that love to wash over them.

On the other hand, you show me a person who believes God's love is enough. You show me a person who believes they are eternally loved by the Eternal Lover, and most likely, I'll be able to show you somebody very willing to step forward to serve, to give, to love, to share. I'll show you somebody who's free.

Started out talking about my morning shower. What it used to be. What it is now.

Next time you take your shower, I presume that will be later today, or tomorrow, let's hope it's at least by tomorrow, [laughter] next time you take your shower, let it be much more than a shower.

Chapter 8

23rd Sunday of Ordinary Time, September 9, 2001

We can do nothin' and feel bad. We can do nothin' and be cynical. We can do nothin' and be apathetic. Or, we can come together, learn, make choices, and do something. And remember, doing something is very different than doing nothing. Even doing a small something is very different than doing nothing.

- Father Greg Tolaas

Gospel Reading

Luke 14: 25-33

²⁵ Once when large crowds of people were going along with Jesus, he turned and said to them, ²⁶ "Those who come to me cannot be my disciples unless they love me more than they love father and mother, wife and children, brothers and sisters, and themselves as well. ²⁷ Those who do not carry their own cross and come after me cannot be my disciples. ²⁸ If one of you is planning to build a tower, you sit down first and figure out what it will cost, to see if you have enough money to finish the job. ²⁹ If you don't, you will not be able to finish the tower after laying the

foundation; and all who see what happened will make fun of you. [30] "You began to build but can't finish the job!," they will say. [31] If a king goes out with ten thousand men to fight another king who comes against him with twenty thousand men, he will sit down first and decide if he is strong enough to face that other king. [32] If he isn't, he will send messengers to meet the other king to ask for terms of peace while he is still a long way off. [33] "In the same way," concluded Jesus, "none of you can be my disciple unless you give up everything you have."

Homily

I think I might have been in second grade or third grade, when we were having a little summer supper one night, and I was showing my muscles to my family. And then I said, "Dad, I wanna see how big your muscle is." He said, "All right, son," and he pulled up his sleeve and he showed me a big, strong arm and I thought, wow that is impressive.

And I said, "Mom, I wanna see your muscle." My mother was about 100 pounds, five foot one, maybe five foot two, kind of wirey. And she said, "Okay." And she pulled up her sleeve and she showed this bulging muscle. I was so impressed. I thought, my God, that's a big bump in my mother's arm! This was not this little kind of fitness-club thing, where "aren't I toned?" but skinny. This was just muscle. And I was very very proud of that in her.

Well then, in third grade, I would come and go from school, and there was a kid whose first name I do not remember, but his last name was Duffy. And this kid was in the seventh grade. He liked to pound the crap out of me, comin' home from school, or goin' to school. And I was no match for him and I would go down Stanford Avenue or I'd go down Wellesley or I'd go through the alleys, trying to avoid this kid, but he would find me. And he would punch me up.

So I was home one day at lunch and I was cryin' about this and so forth, and my mom, very protective, said, "I'm gonna follow you back to school for a few days." So she was following me back to school, and out comes Duffy. And he's got that kind of sadistic smile, like I'm gonna pulp this kid one more time. And my mother comes tearing up the street from about fifty yards away. She grabs this kid, who was taller than she was, and she said, "Don't you ever touch my kid again! And don't you touch any kid in this neighborhood. Do you understand me?" [laughter]

"Blubber, blubber, blubber."

He got the drift. And in those days, I guess you could grab and smack a kid. It was okay. [laughter]

Duffy never bothered me again. And I had this sense that my mother was my protector, my advocate, the one who would stand up for me at any price, and gave me a sense of confidence. And the message was, "Don't mess with my kid." And "Don't mess with my mom."

Very curiously, it was not even two years later, in the complications of childbirth, that my mother, in a crisis, said to the doctors, "Save my baby first. And then save me. I have five children at home." And she did not live through that birth. And in that choice of sacrifice, gave her life. What a parent won't do for their children is amazing, when they are good parents.

Today's Gospel is not an easy gospel. Today's Gospel is the gospel you love to hate. A message like whoever does not carry his or her own cross, and come after me, cannot be my disciple. And at the very end of the reading, Jesus says, "Anyone who does not renounce all his or her possessions, [not some of your possessions, but renounce all your possessions] cannot be my disciple."

Those two lines make me nervous. Those two lines remind

me how gutless I am at times. Well-intended, little follow-through. But Jesus, realizing in his own heart that the road to Jerusalem and his own obedience to the Father was hard work. It cost him everything. It was not a part-time job. It was his passion from His heart to bring about the kingdom, and it came with great price, and great eventual price.

Jesus is setting us straight to say: If you wanna be my disciples, you better be detached from the world. If you wanna be my disciples, you better know that it may cost you friendship. It may cost you even your family. That God and love of God must be first; all else is subordinate. All else. And your possessions, your possessions, they don't even matter. If they stand in the way, get rid of 'em.

He is giving us the recipe for discipleship, which is not easy. But it is rich.

And then He says to us, "You may need to suffer, even the cross." What does that mean? The cross is obviously a thing of great injustice, scandal, torture, humiliation. You may need to suffer, even that. You may need to pick that up and carry it. And carry it with others whose cross is heavy. Others who suffer injustice. Others who suffer scandal. Others who are tortured in their lives. The cross will be part of discipleship. And if you're like me, you say, "I don't wanna hear that!" And "I don't wanna live that! I want it to be THE GLORY AND THE HONOR, ALLELUIA!"

But it is also the path to Jesus. Somehow, the voice of Jesus demands, demands, a bigger love than we're used to giving. It demands that we be unattached. It demands that we reach beyond our comfort zone. It demands that we grow into a relationship of love and mercy and justice with all.

Now the fact is that most of us, like my mother, are willing to take care of our spouse, and our kids. They're ours. That's where we put our energy.

But very very few of us, very few of us think beyond that. How many of you who are parents, last night, when you went to bed, prayed for each of your children? I hope you did. If you didn't, why didn't you? But even if you prayed for your children last night, how many of you who are parents prayed for the children in the Northside community? The children of Hawthorne? How many of you prayed for the children in Sudan and Liberia, places torn apart by war and hatred, anguish and torture?

Our lives are very little sometimes. We take care of our

own and we are not even conscious of that beyond us.

But Jesus is saying: If you're going to be a disciple, the road is really the road of mercy and the road is the road of justice. And justice means we look around us, and we see what's wrong with this picture? What's wrong with our culture? What's wrong with society? And then we jointly commit ourselves to turn that around.

So, for example, in Hawthorne, how many of us are willing, and this is a serious question, not rhetorical, how many of us in these pews, are willing to say: I want to be a part of an effort that makes this neighborhood safer? I want to know these neighbors and these children and their names, and be in some kind of relationship with them, so that I can be an advocate for a safer neighborhood. A place where children can be happy. I want to work for a kind of society where everybody has a voice, everybody has enough to eat, everybody has a safe shelter. There are children living in houses you cannot imagine, despite the fact that the façade doesn't look too bad outside.

For us to say, "Lord, what can I do?" and more importantly, "Lord, what can we do?" You can't do it alone. I can't do it alone. Melissa can't do it alone. Art can't do it alone. But, jointly we can do it. Not only just as a church, but a church in conjunction with our neighbors, and with renters, and homeowners. A church in conjunction with a brand new school. A church in conjunction with the police and the partnership that we have in this neighborhood. To heal and make this a more loving, livable place.

How dare we return to our homes in the suburbs or in Como Park or in Mac-Grove of St. Paul, or in Kenwood, or wherever we live? How dare we not pray for the children of Hawthorne? And, more boldly, how dare we do nothing for those who suffer?

In the next few weeks, we're going to have a little institute on Social Justice, offered at our church. For three Thursday nights, September 20th, 27th, and October 4th. It is designed to give insight and clarity to us about what social justice and the work of discipleship really is about. And then, very practically, to help us know how we want to do that. And how we want to do that, not for our neighbors, but with our neighbors. They will be invited too. And for us then, to create small or large action plans, to say, this is what we're going to work on to improve and heal our neighborhood and our city and our world.

We can do nothin' and feel bad. We can do nothin' and be cynical. We can do nothin' and be apathetic. Or, we can come together, learn, make choices, and do something. And remember, doing something is very different than doing nothing. Even doing a small something is very different than doing nothing.

So you are invited, every one of you, invited to come on those three Thursday nights. I hope we have fifty, sixty people who can come together and say, "What does social justice look like for this community and this neighborhood, that we can live out in our lives?

What do the prophets say about justice? What does Jesus say about justice, and how do we do it together in 2001? All are invited. Who will come?

Jesus says discipleship and the work of the gospel happens at great cost. At great price. Who among us will come forward to be disciples truly and intentionally? Who among us will do the work of gospel compassion and gospel justice?

Remember, discipleship happens at a great price. It also happens to be the great prize.

Chapter 9

24th Sunday of Ordinary Time, September 16, 2001

(Post 9-11 Homily)

We need to pray, and pray some more, and pray some more, as a nation, and discern what to do. And then we need to act, and we need to act with justice and not vengeance. We need to believe, as we sit in this room this morning that our love is bigger than our hate, that our hope is deeper than our despair, that our faith will lead us to wisdom.

- Father Greg Tolaas

Gospel Reading

Luke 15:1-32

[1] One day when many tax collectors and other outcasts came to listen to Jesus, [2] the Pharisees and the teachers of the Law started grumbling, "This man welcomes outcasts and even eats with them!" [3] So Jesus told them this parable:

[4] "Suppose one of you has a hundred sheep and loses one of them - what do you do? You leave the other ninety-nine sheep in the pasture and go looking for the one that got lost until you find it. [5] When you find it, you are so happy that you put it on your shoulders [6] and carry it

back home. Then you call your friends and neighbors together and say to them, 'I am so happy I found my lost sheep. Let us celebrate!' [7] In the same way, I tell you, there will be more joy in heaven over one sinner who repents than over ninety-nine respectable people who do not need to repent.

[8] "Or suppose a woman who has ten silver coins loses one of them - what does she do? She lights a lamp, sweeps her house, and looks carefully everywhere until she finds it. [9] When she finds it, she calls her friends and neighbors together, and says to them, 'I am so happy I found the coin I lost. Let us celebrate!' [10] In the same way, I tell you, the angels of God rejoice over one sinner who repents."

[11] Jesus went on to say, "There was a man who had two sons. [12] The younger one said to him, 'Father, give me my share of the property now.' So the man divided his property between his two sons. [13] After a few days the younger son sold his part of the property and left home with the money. He went to a country far away, where he wasted his money in reckless living. [14] He spent everything he had. Then a severe famine spread over that country, and he was left without a thing. [15] So he went to work for one of the citizens of that country,

who sent him out to his farm to take care of the pigs. [16] He wished he could fill himself with the bean pods the pigs ate, but no one gave him anything to eat. [17] At last he came to his senses and said, 'All my father's hired workers have more than they can eat, and here I am about to starve! [18] I will get up and go to my father and say, "Father, I have sinned against God and against you. [19] I am no longer fit to be called your son; treat me as one of your hired workers. [20] So he got up and started back to his father.

"He was still a long way from home when his father saw him; his heart was filled with pity, and he ran, threw his arms around his son and kissed him. [21] 'Father,' the son said, 'I have sinned against God and against you. I am no longer fit to be called your son.' [22] But the father called to his servants. 'Hurry!' he said. 'Bring the best robe and put it on him Put a ring on his finger and shoes on his feet. [23] Then go and get the prize calf and kill it, and let us celebrate with a feast! [24] For this son of mine was dead, but now he is alive; he was lost, but now he has been found.' And so the feasting began.

[25] "In the meantime the older son was out in the field. On his way back, when he came close to the house, he heard the music and dancing. [26] So he called one of the

servants and asked him, 'What's going on?' ²⁷ 'Your brother has come back home,' the servant answered, 'and your father has killed the prize calf, because he got him back safe and sound.' ²⁸ The older brother was so angry that he would not go into the house; so his father came out and begged him to come in. ²⁹ But he spoke back to his father, 'Look, all these years I have worked for you like a slave, and I have never disobeyed your orders. What have you given me? Not even a goat for me to have a feast with my friends! ³⁰ But this son of yours wasted all your property on prostitutes, and when he comes back home, you kill the prize calf for him!' ³¹ 'My son,' the father answered, 'you are always here with me, and everything I have is yours. ³² But we had to celebrate and be happy because your brother was dead, but now he is alive; he was lost, but now he has been found.'"

Homily

It's been strange to ask people this week, "How are you?" And have them say. "Great!" "Good!" And when people have asked me, I have been unable to say, "Good" or "Fine." And never, "Great." It has been a week of Hell.

Last night I watched an airplane flying over the house where I had gathered for the birthday party of my friend who is 86 and has cancer. He's a very dear man, looks terribly thin. I looked up at that airplane and I thought, "I will never look up into the sky at the underbelly of an airplane and think the same thing again." I saw a potential weapon flying right over the house. Or I think of any number of snipits and snapshots and sound bites that we have listened to. This morning again, talking about the priest, fire chaplain who died. How loving he was. How giving he was. How igniting his spirit was. What kindness he had. And I found out the other day, he was, of all things, also gay. This loving man, very dead, because he chose to love.

I can't imagine which fills each of your hearts this week. At first it's horror and maybe hatred and befuddlement and fear and every kind of emotion. And it's kind of strange, cuz three days later, the emotions shift a bit. And ten days later, the emotions shift a lot more and sometimes we're back to "great." But it has been something that tears at the heart, something that fills us with fear and with rage, at best.

Yet we gather here this morning, most of us, as Americans, most of us also as Christians. It is important that we be very careful not to forget. It is very important that we not simply become lazy of spirit and apathetic about what has happened. And it is equally important that we not give way simply to our rage.

We need to pray, and pray some more, and pray some more, as a nation, and discern what to do. And then we need to act, and we need to act with justice and not vengeance. We need to believe, as we sit in this room this morning. that our love is bigger than our hate, that our hope is deeper than our despair, that our faith will lead us to wisdom.

We also need to remember today, and sometimes this is tough for us, as we've seen on the news, that God loves all his Christian children. And God loves all his Muslim children. God loves all his Muslim children and we also need to remember, I think, foremost, that terrorism is always, always wrong. It was wrong when it happened to us this week, and it would be wrong for us ever to terrorize another people.

So we need to pray to have the mind of God, and equally important, we need to pray to have the heart of God.

We listened to that First Reading today from Exodus. God is saying, "You have been an unfaithful people and I'm telling you: Moses, I'm bringin' 'em down! I will not put up with their unfaithfulness. My wrath is true."

And we say: my God, was that the wrath of God that happened this week? Someone in the Taliban might say so, yes. Allah asked us to do this. But let me be clear, the wrath of God is always rooted in justice, and in mercy, and in mercy, and always rooted in love. The way that you can know what happened this past week is not of God is that it was not rooted in justice. It was not rooted in mercy. And it was, in no way, an act of love.

So if we are to be like God and have the mind of God and the heart of God, even in seeking justice, not vengeance, even in seeking justice, we must remember mercy, we must pray for wisdom, and we must be rooted, not in hate, tempting as that is, and I have felt hate this week, I don't know about you. We must be rooted in love.

Let's turn to that Gospel today. My God, what a gospel! Three scenarios. First scenario, there is a lost sheep out there. And the Shepherd, when he finds the lost sheep, the one lost sheep, however naughty that sheep was, however inattentive, it had split from the flock, or got lost, whatever it was, that shepherd rejoices. When the woman finds her lost coin, she rejoices. And most importantly, in the final story, full of mercy, this unconditional mercy, the father who could rub it is his son's face, simply rejoices.

Three times, rejoice, rejoice, rejoice.

What was lost has been found. How do we deal with that? How do we deal, as Christian Americans, with that Gospel because there's a part of us that wants next week to not look about mercy, next week to not feel like forgiveness. But I need to approach next week and the next week and the next week as a Christian person. And the Gospel says you better be about forgiveness and you better be about mercy, along with your justice.

I believe God wants to find anyone who is lost, even Bin Laden. God wants to find anyone who is lost. He wants to bring that lost sheep back to the fold. And then he wants to show justice and mercy to his lost sheep, whether Christian or Jewish, Hindu or Muslim. And that prayer will guide us. I'm kind of nervous about sayin' this, but I echo the words of Archbishop Flynn. Archbishop Flynn said this week, "While we must do justice, whatever that looks like, and while we must come to justice, prayerfully, we also need to ask them the question. Why do you hate us? Why do you detest us?"

They are not simply maniacs, necessarily. There is something. Is it in our culture? Is it in our sinful way of life and our lack of morals? Is it in our finances? What is it about us that you hate? And to be able to imagine for a moment sitting down at the table, with people and talking and finding answers to those questions so that terrorism will not be an option, because terrorism can never ever,

ever, be an option. To remember that terrorism is not Christian and terrorism is not Muslim.

We all use the phrase, Islamic Terrorists. I heard a Pakistani say the other night, on the news, "Terrorists are terrorists." Terrorists are not acting Christian and they are not acting Muslim. Read the Koran and the tenant to the same God we believe in, as you believe in. But even there, to somehow believe that there might be a sliver or more than a sliver of a chance of sitting down, in diplomacy, to say what is it about us and what is it about you that needs to change so that we might be a global community?

I believe that God believes in every human being. And if we take today's gospel story and if we say all the nations of the world have pretty much come together here, except Afghanistan. Is Afghanistan, perhaps, the lost sheep out there in the desert? If it is, then you can be sure that our Shepherd is looking to draw the lost sheep into the fold. To say, "Come to the table. Come and talk. Come and be reconciled. Come and be unified."

In my world, says the shepherd, there is one flock and I will never be happy until all my sheep are together. I will not settle for left and right. I do not like Northern Ireland, Catholic and Protestant. I do not believe in the hatred of

Jews and Palestinians in Jerusalem. I believe in one flock, one people. I am one God. My name is Love. So must your name be Love.

Now for those of us who think that Bin Laden is simply a maniac, and sometimes I think that, and sometimes I don't know what I think. I turn us to St. Paul. We are comforted today. Paul says to dear Timothy: Timothy, I was so hateful, I was so hurtful. I persecuted freely. I was arrogant and I was ignorant. And then I was touched by the love of God and the face of Jesus, and the power of the Spirit. And I changed. I changed.

That leads me to believe that if the Holy Spirit is real, that Spirit will never give up on any of us, Muslim or Christian, Arab or Jew, American or something else. That same Spirit is saying; I will work and I will love. And I will love until you come together. When will you listen? When will you be docile to my invitation?

And right now, I don't want to be docile. Right now, I want to drop some bombs. Drop bombs on what? Drop bombs on who? We don't even know where to drop the bombs. The answer might be eventually, or in diplomacy, and certainly in love.

Today, I pray for me and my heart, which is capable of hatred. And I pray for you. And I pray for our president and every world leader. And I pray for the terrorists who absolutely need our prayers. And I pray for Bin Laden. And I pray for anyone who is lost and driven by hate. Because I believe that this crazy Gospel and this unbelievable Jesus Christ really did have the only answer. And most of us still don't get it.

This Gospel today demands that I and you believe in mercy, believe in reconciliation, along with justice. This Gospel demands that we try to bring every sheep back into one flock. For only when the very last lost sheep is found, only when the flock is one and no one is missing, only when there is unity and healing, only then, will my Shepherd rejoice.

Chapter 10

26th Sunday of Ordinary Time, September 30, 2001

For those of you who lounge on your couches, taking care of you, flipping the remote, and never gettin' off the couch, for those of you who are in your own comfort, or in your own self malaise, wake up! Step out! Be there for someone else.

- Father Greg Tolaas

Gospel Reading

Luke 16: 19-31

[19] There was once a rich man who dressed in the most expensive clothes and lived in great luxury every day. [20] There was also a poor man named Lazarus, covered with sores, who used to be brought to the rich man's door, [21] hoping to eat the bits of food that fell from the rich man's table. Even the dogs would come and lick his sores. [22] The poor man died and was carried by the angels to sit beside Abraham at the feast in heaven. The rich man died and was buried, [23] and in Hades, where he was in great pain, he looked up and saw Abraham, far away, with Lazarus at his side. [24] So he called out,

'Father Abraham! Take pity on me, and send Lazarus to dip his finger in some water and cool off my tongue, because I am in great pain in this fire!' ²⁵ But Abraham said, 'Remember, my son, that in your lifetime you were given all the good things, while Lazarus got all the bad things. But now he is enjoying himself here, while you are in pain. ²⁶ Besides all that, there is a deep pit lying between us, so that those who want to cross over from here to you cannot do so, nor can anyone cross over to us from where you are.' ²⁷ The rich man said, 'Then I beg you, father Abraham, send Lazarus to my father's house, ²⁸ where I have five brothers. Let him go and warn them so that they, at least, will not come to this place of pain.' ²⁹ Abraham said, 'Your brothers have Moses and the prophets to warn them; your brothers should listen to what they say.' ³⁰ The rich man answered, 'That is not enough, father Abraham! But if someone were to rise from death and go to them, then they would turn from their sins.' ³¹ But Abraham said, 'If they will not listen to Moses and the prophets, they will not be convinced even if someone were to rise from death.'"

Homily

On the one hand I want to thank you for being very hospitable last weekend to my friend, Father Jim Smith, Pastor of our partner church at Transfiguration. But this week I have heard quite a bit of, "Oh, we just love Father Jim".

"Oh, that Father Jim was so nice".

"Oh, he gave a good homily."

"Oh, he's so cute."
Father Jim. Father Jim. Father Jim.

I'm tired. [laughter] You will never see him again. [laughter].

That Father Doug came here a few years ago and you've never seen him again. You liked him a lot too.

Never push my buttons. Please.

Terrorism is abuse at its very worst. We still taste it in our mouths. We still taste it in our hearts. It was difficult for me even this morning to look at more footage where there's still smoke coming up out of this ash and rubble! The fruit of an evil hatred. Terrorism is always, always evil, never, ever from God or Allah.

In its micro, I also was visited by the notion of abuse this past week. I don't know if you saw it on the news, but there was a woman in Afghanistan and it showed footage. Her veil had slipped from her face for a moment. And a man, walking along, who had a club, he just starts to beat her. And he beat her and he beat her and she's screaming and she's falling to the ground. And he's beating her on the ground. And I was so filled with ugliness and rage.

Abuse, a man striking a woman, with a stick, multiple times. Abuse is never, ever, ever, from God or of God.

As you know, Hilary works in our neighborhood. And we are engaged in our neighborhood. She reported very sadly one day of a house full of children and full of a multiplicity of dogs. Dogs who were not let out. Feces around the house. Filth. Vermin. Radical neglect. Children living in squalor. That kind of neglect is never, ever from God.

So, what do we do with September 11th, 2001? What do we do when we see the footage of a young woman being beaten, who knows – to death or not to death, because her veil slipped from her face? What do we do with the anger and the rage and the despair and the distance? What do we do with the fear and the anxiety and the loss of innocence and the loss of trust? What happens to us because of such a day? Do I leave September 11th more able to hate than I did on the 10th? Or do I live, after September 11th, more able to love than on the 10th?

It's an important question. Because those events, whether macro abuse or micro abuse, those events, touch us. And they either destroy our spirit and make us isolate ourselves and pull inward and just take care of me and just take care of mine and trust nobody. And I'm not reachin' out and I'm not steppin' out of my comfort zone, small and safe. Or a date like September 11th makes us decide to be transformed. Forever changed! Absolutely, forever changed! But changed to say, "I will choose to be more loving, more invested, more involved, more risky! I will choose to send my healing power and our healing power into this world to make a difference so that abuse and neglect and terrorism are not so viable, and don't even exist." That's the two choices. To insulate, isolate, and self protect, or to invest and step out, in love, and with the holy anger at times, to say, "I and we will make a difference." Those are our choices.

The story today is interesting. A rich man who ate sumptuously, what a great word, huh? Who ate sumptuously every day. Lazarus, open sores, dogs licking his sores, begging to be noticed, begging for a bit of help. Both die. One in the heart of Abraham, one in the bosom of Abraham; one in the flames and torment that he had sown for himself. And it's interesting, even in death, the rich man is still saying, "Father Abraham, tell Lazarus to bring me some water." He still felt he was entitled. He still felt that the poor were there to kind of take care of him. Well then at least send Lazarus to talk to my brothers.

And Father Abraham is saying: Don't you get it? You don't get it. Your life must not be all about you taking care of you. Your life was to be such that you opened your eyes and saw what was around you. Your life was to be such that you paid attention to Lazarus, that you paid attention to all the Lazaruses out there and had you noticed him and had you made some different choices, to step outside of your sumptuous life, had you given yourself to the good or to the common good, you too would be in my bosom and not in the torment you sowed for yourself."

The message is clear to us. The prophet Amos says, "For those of you who spend your life drinking wine from bowls," What an image! For those of you who lounge on your couches, taking care of you, flipping the remote, and never gettin' off the couch, for those of you who are in your own comfort, or in your own self malaise, wake up! Step out! Be there for someone else. And even in these days that have happened, it's so easy to be the armchair quarterback. Well, this is what happened, this is what we gotta do. We gotta get in there; we gotta get the terrorists, and so forth. I'm afraid we're gonna have to leave some of that up to the planners, in our government, and our leaders. Though we can pray for them and we can have whatever voice is possible.

But what we do have, is we do have our back yard. And in our backyard there is some neglect. And there is plenty of human pain. And there is a need for us to invest our energies to say: You know what, if Hawthorne and Jordan and these neighborhoods look different, the world is different.

If I care for my family with great care, and if I reach out beyond my family, to care for my parishioners, and my neighbors, then we are all different. We are blessed because of that. When the world changes a little, the whole world changes. That's how it happens.

I know so many people are sayin' I'm overwhelmed by what happened, I'm overwhelmed by the terrorism, but I can't do anything. And I want to stand here today to say to you, "Doing something, however small, doing something, is very different than doing nothing. Never forget that. Doing one small thing is very different than doing nothing."

When is the last time any of us called our great aunt so and so, who's in a nursing home, never see her, never really make the visit, always gonna, gonna, gonna, woulda, coulda, shoulda. But she never really gets the visit or the card or the phone call.

Step out.

When is the last time we thought, gee, it would be nice to volunteer with a child in the neighborhood, or be a

Compassionate Companion for a kid, but we never make the call. Woulda, coulda, shoulda. Thank God for those who make the call! One kid at a time. If one child reads because you taught him to read, their whole world will be different. If one child grows up sayin', "I am somebody. I am special. I am loved. I have a world of possibility," you have changed that child's whole future. You have changed the whole world.

To step out of our comfort zone because we notice Lazarus, wherever he or she is, that's what it's about.

I will always hate that September 11th, 2001 happened. I will always hate it. It will always go down in history as an evil, tragic day. But out of those ashes, and out of that horror, comes either destruction of ourselves or the re-creation of ourselves.

I invite us today to make new choices, to step out, to make the phone call, to volunteer somewhere, somehow.

I'll tell you a little story. Sometimes I think, I've been treadin' here on the old hamster wheel for four years now and you wonder if you make any difference at all. Well we got these hoops out here. And most of you don't have the enjoyment of seeing that every evening there's 30, 40, sometimes 50 young people out there playin' hoops. It's just fantastic! That's 50 kids not out on the street, bored. But they do drive you a little crazy cuz when they jump, they like to hang on the hoop! And that gets Father a little upset. And so I'm kind of a screaming fool out the window sometimes. And one day, I was in my garden here and a teenager went Boooom; and I see him hangin' out there and I can't believe it and say, "Hey! Get off that hoop!" Because he was from here to about the back of the church. And he looks at me and he says, "Can you ask that nicely?" [laughter].

Well, he was buried yesterday. [laughter] It was a quick and painless death. [laughter] I couldn't believe it! And I said, "Well, let me rephrase it, "I'm really sorry that I yelled and lost my temper, but I see this happen 30 times a night and sometimes it gets on my nerves."

And he said, "It's the first time I did it, and I won't do it, but thanks for asking nicely. That's cool." [laughter] I thought one moment, one teenager, great manners, great kid, good moment for me.

Those teens need somebody who gives a rip about them. We have a few volunteers with our teens. We could have a dozen. That part's up to you. That part's up to me.

Let's take a moment of quiet, to make decisions, personally, and as a community. Will we see Lazarus? When we see Lazarus, will we notice and do something? And do we wish to live in the torment of our own selfishness? Or in the bosom of Abraham? And better yet, the heart of God?

Chapter 11

27th Sunday of Ordinary Time, October 7, 2001

But I'm not going to spend the rest of my life standing back, waiting to see if something appeals to me enough where I might give a bit of my time, maybe. I'll think about it. That's not a way to do life and it's not a posture of gratitude. That is selfishness; all about me takin' care of me, in case something funner comes along.

- Father Greg Tolaas

Gospel Reading

Luke 17:5-10

⁵ The apostles said to the Lord, "Make our faith greater."

⁶ The Lord answered, "If you had faith as big as a mustard seed, you could say to this mulberry tree, 'Pull yourself up by the roots and plant yourself in the sea!' and it would obey you.

⁷ "Suppose one of you has a servant who is plowing or looking after the sheep. When he comes in from the field, do you tell him to hurry along and eat his meal? ⁸ Of course not! Instead, you say to him, 'Get my supper

ready, then put on your apron and wait on me while I eat and drink; after that you may have your meal.' [9] The servant does not deserve thanks for obeying order, does he? [10] It is the same with you; when you have done all you have been told to do, say, 'We are ordinary servants, we have only done our duty.'

Homily

Do you know how you know when you're getting old? You know you're getting old when you start looking at people younger than you, a generation younger than you, and you start saying, "These kids nowadays are so mouthy, so disrespectful; they think they're entitled to everything."

We look at our friends' kids. Sometimes we even look at our grandkids. We look at youth and we say they're ungrateful. They're demanding. They're mouthy to their parents. I have friends whose kids I've heard say, "Shut up" to their parents and I thought to myself, when I was a kid, if I had said "shut up" to my parents, I would have no lips. I might have no face, for all I know. It would have been out of the question to be mouthy like that to a parent. Oftentimes we wonder why our kids seem so entitled. They think that everything they got, they got comin' to them. It doesn't really matter if you're a rich kid, a middle class kid, or a poor kid. There's this sense that I'm entitled to everything that you gave me. And I'm entitled to more than what you've given to me. And it does not spawn, in a child or in anybody, a sense of gratitude.

I think many of us live our lives, feeling that God owes us an easy life. God owes us an abundant life. We look at what we have. It's easy to look around and say, "Why didn't I get this?" or "Why am I sick?" or "Why does this happen to me?" And "My life is so hard," and "People have picked on me," and "I'm a victim." Some of us live our whole lives feeling like, "I'm a victim."

I could stand up here today and tell you at times, that I hate my life. I could tell you about my CF for 45 years. I could tell you about my shut-down pancreas and my diabetes. I could tell you about my kidney disease, which is whackin' out all over the place. I could tell you about my high blood pressure and all my meds. I could tell you that when my mother died, my father died, my sister died, my sister died. And I have a nasty life!

And you get to a certain point where you're either gonna live with this sense that I have gotten the short straw all my life, or you decide to look through different eyes, with perspective. The fact is my life is blessed. I am very loved by many people. I had wonderful parents. I have, every day of my life, had enough to eat. I was sent to wonderful schools and was allowed to have education, and education, and more education. I have traveled the world. I've been to Europe twelve times? I don't know how many times. I am blessed.

I am blessed with a living faith. I am blessed with a wonderful community of faith. I am blessed with meaningful work. I am blessed that I get up and I can see. I am blessed cuz I can walk and Sue cannot. I am so blessed. And I can either look at my life and say, "I got the short straw and my life sucks," (excuse my language.) or I can say, "I have been blessed and blessed and blessed and blessed."

You've met the kind of person who lives their life always sayin', "Short straw, poor me. God never took care of me. God never heard my prayer."

"How long, O Lord" said the First Reading.

And then you meet people, who, no matter what has happened in their lives, no matter what hardships have been there, somehow, they find the blessing. And all we need to do is look around. You know what? Most of us in this church ate this morning, if we wanted to, will eat at noon if we want to, and we'll eat tonight!

I've been watchin' the news. So have you. What is it like to be an Afghan woman in a refugee camp in Pakistan, squatting over a fire, wondering if there's enough to feed your infected children, who have snot on their nose, and mosquitoes all over their face? That's hardship. I have never been asked to live that by life. Cuz I am blessed. And so are you. Each of us radically blessed. And when we realize that we are blessed, then it isn't so hard to be a servant of the Master, cuz we say, "The Master loves me. The Master has given me health. The Master has given me breath. The Master is wrapping me in love."

And if I have the faith, even a tiny portion of faith, I would be overwhelmed by how loved I am. I would be overwhelmed by how blessed I am. And then it's much easier to say, "Lord, do with me what you will, cuz I'm doin' it out of a response of gratitude. I'm doin' it knowin' how blessed I am!" Instead of sayin' "I don't really feel like volunteering. I'm not going to step out of myself. I'm not givin' any money to the church. And nobody really has bothered to pay attention to me."

We can gripe our whole life away. And I've met people who do. It's so tiring. Or we can say, "Because I am so loved, so gifted, so cared for, so fed, so nourished, I will give to my Master, and I will do what is asked of me. And if it means scrubbing floors, I'll scrub floors. If it means runnin' a nation, I'll run a nation. If it means being a surgeon, I'll use my hands to heal. If it means bein' a priest, I'll be a priest! If it means teaching small children to read, I will find that a privilege."

But I'm not going to spend the rest of my life standing back, waiting to see if something appeals to me enough where I might give a bit of my time, maybe. I'll think about it. That's not a way to do life and it's not a posture of gratitude. That is selfishness; all about me takin' care of me, in case something funner comes along.

But when we're blessed, and when we know we're blessed, and when we have a bit of faith, we can say, "Lord, give me faith today." And we wake up the next day and we say, "Lord, give me a bigger portion of faith today." And we wake up the next day and we say, "Give me a portion of your Spirit. Fill my heart with gratitude. Fill my heart with faith to see what you have done for my life." And then, in that gratitude, step out and serve.

The Gospel said today, when we get to the end of our lives, we will say, "We are God's servants. We are the Master's servants. And no matter how much we gave, it was no more than what was asked of us." But another way to look at it is to say, "At the end of our life, if we spent our whole life serving and if we did it knowing we were loved first, always loved, always sustained, always cared for, then it is not hard to do."

This morning, we are gonna have an opportunity fair downstairs, lettin' you know about a bazillion kinds of things goin' on here at St. Philip. If you are a parishioner, and you come here just to get your fix, and you are involved in no ministry whatever, I'm goin' to ask you to rethink that. I don't care if you're eight or eighty-eight. We've got a prayer chain for those who can't get out of the house. We have many wonderful opportunities. Cindy put together a little book. I was reading through it last night, in the bathroom, quite honestly. And I was so touched by the way she puts these words together about a multiplicity of things to do. I'm not asking you to do ten things. But I'm also sayin' don't do no thing. Don't do nothin'.

This is an amazing faith community because people, who know they are blessed, are learning, day after day, to reach out beyond themselves, to love God's world, cuz we've been loved first. At the end of our life, we'll be able to say, "I was a loved servant, with a loving Master. I did no more than I was privileged to do."

Chapter 12

30th Sunday of Ordinary Time, October 28, 2001

*There is a great danger when we are full of ourself; and there is
a great danger when we say I am nothing; I am nothing; I am
nothing. And too many of us, in every congregation, have sold
ourselves short. We don't minister or we don't serve or we don't
lay hands on people, cuz we think we got nothin' to give!*

- Father Greg Tolaas

Gospel Reading

Luke 18: 9-14

[9] Jesus also told this parable to people who were sure of their own goodness and despised everybody else. [10] "Once there were two men who went up to the Temple to pray: one was a Pharisee, the other a tax collector. [11] The Pharisee stood apart by himself and prayed, 'I thank you, God, that I am not greedy, dishonest, or an adulterer, like everybody else. I thank you that I am not like that tax collector over there. [12] I fast two days a week, and I give you one tenth of all my income.' [13] But the tax collector stood at a distance and would not even raise his face to heaven, but beat on his breast and

said, 'God, have pity on me, a sinner!' [14] I tell you, said Jesus, 'the tax collector, and not the Pharisee, was in the right with God when he went home. For those who make themselves great will be humbled, and those who humble themselves will be made great.'"

Homily

One of the dangers of preaching often, and aging, is that you forget where you told what story and to whom. And you are fearful that people are going to say, "Oh my God, we've heard all this before." But I always rest in the assumption that a good story is worth repeating.

I may have told you about a friend of mine; his name is Rodney. He is a priest about 38 years old. When he was three years old, his father who worked for the electric company in the state of Nebraska, was up on top of an electrical pole working and he was burned, an electrical burn, and he fell to the ground, 20, 22 feet, whatever it was. And within a couple days, they had to cut off his arms, close to the shoulder. He went on to raise, not only those four children, but they had two more children. And he learned to do his life with prostheses. Two hooks. He can change the oil on the car. He can do tons of things. He will put that hook out to you to shake your hand when he meets you. You're a little surprised, at first. And one day, my friend said to his dad, "Dad, how is it that you are not so bitter about what happened to you. You lost your arms. You lost your hands. Most would say they've lost their life when such a thing happens." And his father had four words to share with him. He was kind of a quiet man. He said to his son:

"Joy is a choice. Joy is a choice."

I want you to take a moment to look seriously, now, at your hands. I want you to look at your hands. I want you to look at them carefully to see what rings you are wearing and why you are wearing them. Look at the tops of your hands. Look at the palms of your hands. Do you have calluses? Are you a house scrubber? From detergents, your hands might be rough or you might be one of those people who guard their hands very carefully, and uses lotion multiple times a day. You might have your nails done with long extensions on them. Or you might bite your nails right down to the grit. What do your hands tell you about your life? What have you done with your hands? Who have you loved with your hands? Who did you slap or strike with your hands?

Our hands are a tremendous, tremendous teacher and gift. Think for a moment, eyes back here. Think for a moment, of the hands in this congregation. I think of Patsy Ryan, who was surprised when her son was born deaf and they learned how to talk sign language as a family. She's very, very fluent. She has used her hands to touch the lives of hundreds of deaf people, and bring them into the world of knowledge and communication. The use of her hands.

I think of Dale Korogi who plays so beautifully and whose fingers can do what my fingers can never do. I've tried. He's heard me play. It's not pretty. I play, "Blowin' in the Wind" with that rolling left hand. And he rolls his eyes and says nothing. But, what a gift, to lead us to pray better because of the beauty comin' out of what his hands can do.

Or I think of Bill Payne, who is a skilled and gifted surgeon, who looks down and puts veins together with veins as a gifted vascular surgeon, or transplants organs, so people are alive because of what his hands can do.

Or I think of Mary Miezwa, who has always hated her hands. She says, "My hands are too big." Mary is a very hard worker. And Fran, her sister. And the love they have done in cleaning homes, caring for families and cleaning my rectory when it's filthy. Lovingly comin' in and sayin' we'll get down on our hands and our knees and scrub your floors, out of love.

I think of the hands that are all over in this assembly. How many of you have, with your hands, made a thousand meals, or 10,000 meals and chose to do it with love? How many of you have held the hand of a child in this neighborhood, as you bring them up to Kids' Club or walked them home. Or hold them in your lap right now, Adam?

Love is a choice.

These hands of ours are such a gift. Or such a weapon. Look at your hands. And love what you have done with them.

I've been frustrated lately because of the multiplicity of health issues that I'm dealing with, and I was at the doctor the other day, and he said to me, "Your kidney function is less than it was six months ago. You're at about 30% now." And I was really angry and sad and frightened to hear that. I was at 50% a year and a half ago. And I'm nervous about losing my kidneys.

And so I ran into dear Sr. Mary Angela on Friday. She's sittin' right here with her eyes shut, deep in prayer listening. [laughter] And Angela said to me. [laughter]. Somebody, wake her up! Wake her up! You've been missing this whole talk. She is gifted with very deep prayer and very deep faith and very deep joy. And she said to me very, very clearly, "Tomorrow I'm coming here with some people. We do intercessory. And we're going to be in the neighborhood praying for those who need it. We're going to start on you tomorrow. Be ready at 10:00 o'clock."

I thought, Oh my God. I don't know what this means. I don't know if I wanna do that. I'm a little sophisticated for havin' people just lay their hands on me and pray. And these might be charismatics, you know, and that really gets wild. And they were and it did. [laughter] I walk in and she's got these six women there. I don't know their names. I still don't know their names. I never got their names. And they sit me down in a chair and they laid hands on me. And part of me thought, wait, wait, wait, I'm the priest, and I do the anointing. Then part of me said, "No. I am somebody in need of healing and they are here to pray." And utterly un-self-consciously, those women prayed for 45, 50 minutes over me, incredibly, with words of scripture, and I could feel the movement of love coming through their fingertips into my body. And at one point one of the women said, "We need to anoint him. He is here doing an important work on the Northside where faith must be shared with people living in despair and poverty and struggle and drugs. We need to anoint him." All right; anoint me. And so they took the oil and they anointed me on my head and on my eyes, and on my lips, and on my ears, and on my hands. And then they started taking my shoes and socks off. And I thought, okay, let's go. Head to toes. And this woman is down, praying as she's holding my feet, and in the midst of it, I knew God was present.

Now, I don't believe in magic. Healing isn't about magic. Healing is about what happens when we give ourselves to love, when we give ourselves to the work of Jesus, when we give ourselves to layin' our hands on each other and entering into each other's lives. And those women (like I said, I don't know what their names were); but I was tellin' John about it a little later in the house, and he said, "well maybe they were angels." And I kind of smiled. And about a half hour later I looked out into the parking lot and one of them had driven a great big Suburban; about four or five of them had been in the Suburban. And they were now out over the neighborhood, visiting or praying, or just walking, silently praying. I don't know. But I looked at the license plate and it said, "RC ANGEL on the license plate and I smiled and said well, maybe they were angels, who drive a big fat Suburban from Elk River. [laughter]

If you look at the scriptures today, if you look at that Gospel today, we have two characters. One is full of himself. He's very sophisticated. He's very intellectual. He's financially got some means. He's full of himself. "Aren't I wonderful? I am above others; certainly above sinners. I'm above doing menial tasks." The other one is so full of humiliation, that he can only strike his breast and say, "God, I am nothing before you."

But the reality is this.

There is a great danger when we are full of ourself; and there is a great danger when we say I am nothing; I am nothing; I am nothing. And too many of us, in every congregation, have sold ourselves short. We don't minister or we don't serve or we don't lay hands on people, cuz we think we got nothin' to give!

The fact is, if we are willing to open ourselves up, God can move through us to love, and teach, and heal, and bake and cook, and care for one another in a thousand different ways. If you are called to be a wonderful surgeon, then do it, and do it with love. If you are called to be a priest, and lay your hands on people and offer them the prayer of the sacraments, do it with love. And if you are called to scrub toilets, or wipe somebody's rear end, day in and day out, because you've been called to do it with love, then do it with love. The what doesn't matter so much. What does matter is that we step outside of ourselves and say. "God, you are in me. You are alive in me. And You can use me and us to change the world."

Stop passin' the buck, cuz you're above it. And stop passin' the buck cuz you think you're nothin'. We are all loved, all anointed. We could all be layin' hands on people who are feelin' depressed, and despairing, lonely, and aged.

When was the last time one of us bothered to visit a parishioner or an elderly relation in the nursing home? To just hold their hand and be with them for an hour. We're so busy, aren't we? We're too busy. We're too full of ourselves sometimes.

Paul says today in the scriptures, "I am being poured out like a libation. I have run the race. I have given all that I can give. The power of God has been in me. I have let Him move through me, and I'm nearing the end of the race. But I have fought the good fight. I have run the race. God has been with me."

Listen to that scripture today, to embrace what you are called to do with your heart, with your gifts, with your time, and with your hands.

It is amazing what healing is experienced when we bother to pray, when we bother to lay hands, when we bother to step outside of ourselves. Take a moment. Look at your hands open in your lap, one more time, and recommit them to the work of love.

Chapter 13

31st Sunday of Ordinary Time, November 4, 2001

The invitation is given to each of us. Free to choose, yes. Free to say no. And I would imagine, most of us, if we don't worship once in a while, or quite regularly, it is because we are so clueless of the immense and tremendous and intimate and tender bond that God holds out to us.

- Father Greg Tolaas

Gospel Reading

Luke 19:1-10

[1] Jesus went on into Jericho and was passing through. [2] There was a chief tax collector there named Zacchaeus, who was rich. [3] He was trying to see who Jesus was, but he was a little man and could not see Jesus because of the crowd. [4] So he ran ahead of the crowd and climbed a sycamore tree to see Jesus, who was going to pass that way. [5] When Jesus came to that place, he looked up and said to Zacchaeus, "Hurry down, Zacchaeus, because I must stay in your house today."

[6] Zacchaeus hurried down and welcomed him with

great joy. [7]All the people who saw it started grumbling, "This man has gone as a guest to the home of a sinner!"

[8]Zacchaeus stood up and said to the Lord, "Listen, sir! I will give half my belongings to the poor, and if I have cheated anyone, I will pay back four times as much."

[9]Jesus said to him, "Salvation has come to this house today, for this man, also, is a descendant of Abraham. The Son of Man came to seek and to save the lost."

Homily

Who was it that you celebrated on Thursday, this week? Who was it that you honored at Eucharist on Thursday, this past week? Many of us might be saying, "What was Thursday, this week?" Thursday was the great feast of All Saints. And my guess is a high majority of Roman Catholics blew it off, or forgot about it. Or said, "I'm very busy with my work." "I have a job. It's fulltime." Or just decided, well you know, "I can't really remember if I'm supposed to be at that one or not." But my guess is that most of us didn't find our way to worship and honor the God and the loved ones who have gone before us who were very faithful.

Sometimes, if I weren't a priest, I'm not sure if I'd show up very faithfully on such Holy Days, cuz I'm a very busy person too, you understand.

I've a rose on the altar. It is reminiscent of my father. He's one of the dead. And when I think back on my dad's life, he had a ghastly amount on his plate. Widowed at 37 years old, with six little kids under age 12 down to newborn; four children with Cystic Fibrosis, sleeping in mist tents. No health insurance. It wasn't provided for catastrophic illness in those days. Money goin' in his right hand, out his left hand in an instant, day after day.

And I remember, even though my dad and I had lots of things to argue about, I think we were both strong willed, at least he was strong willed, one of the things I always observed about him was that he worshipped utterly faithfully.

When we were up at the lake, when he was up at the lake, he always found the way to worship God at the Eucharist. When we were home and we were sayin, "Why do we have to go? I hate it. Monsignor is a drag. He's a bore. It's horrible." He'd say, "We're going." and then he'd say to us, "If you can't give thanks and praise to God for one hour a week for all the blessings you and I have, what's wrong with you? Shame on us."

And I'm going, "My God, our family is hanging on by our toenails. It' crazy! What do you mean, blessed? What do we have to thank God for? This has not been a very fun ride so far."

But he saw his life as blessing. And I remember him sitting us down, and sometimes in tears, he'd be crying with us. We were little. And he'd be saying, "People are sayin' we're not gonna make it. And people suggested that we give up Patty Jo, the infant, cuz you can't possibly raise this infant without a mother." And he'd say, "We are going to make it. We are a family. And I need your help. We will make it." And we'd be cryin' and say, "Okay, we'll help." Tryin' to hang together. But I would watch him in his life and on every Holy Day he would find his way to some downtown church, and maybe some of you did too. It wasn't negotiable. And when he would have those family meetings together, he would say to us, "I don't care about my law office. I don't care about the lake. This house means nothing to me. My cars mean nothing to me. You kids, next to God, are everything in my life."

Next to God, you are everything I have. Next to God, you are my first love. And what I will always carry with me is that my father's first love was not his wife, whom he adored, and was not his six kids, whom he loved sacrificially, his first love was God. And you don't bag God.

The first reading is quite powerful. That first reading reminds us that, in fact, we are kind of nothing. It says, "Before the Lord, the whole universe is as one grain in a balance, or a drop of rain come down from earth. We are small. We are nothing on the one hand. This author of the universe, a universe that goes beyond the galaxies, beyond this solar system, to how many others, we don't know, this God, in whose presence we are tiny and miniscule, says to us: I know you. I love you. I love you. I love you. I know your name, Joe Langel. I know your story. I know every chapter and verse. I know every heartache you've ever had. I know every dream and excitement you've ever had. I know every secret each of you has. I know every longing you have to be whole and to be happy. I know you inside and out and despite your sins, I know you individually and corporately. And bottom line is I love you. I love you. I love you.

And so we are reminded. And God says here: I loathe nothing that I have made. I have made you beautiful. I have made you good. I have loved you and I have made you to love me in return. And in loving me, you must love each other. That's why you're here on earth. Not to be so busy that I got to get to the club or I gotta get to the Aveda Institute, where I went Friday for a really bad haircut, as a matter of fact. A 95-minute haircut.

All the things we've gotta fit in because of our lives on the hamster wheel. And God says: Just stop and let me love you. And once you know how much I love you, you will be at worship.

And what we do on All Saints is we stop for a moment to realize that we carry within us, the faith of our mother or our father. The faith of our grandparents. The faith of this nun in school who mentored us and taught us. I think of you, Meg, with Sister Shirley, what a powerful person she was in your high school years. The people who have loved us along the way and the many who have gone before us, whom we honor and say: I have my faith because you gave it to me. A most precious thing.

And we turn to Zacheus in the Gospel. It says that Zacheus wanted to see Jesus. It doesn't say he had become a disciple. It doesn't say that he was riveted on Jesus. He just wanted to see him. He was a wealthy guy. People basically hated his guts. He was a tax collector. But he wanted to see this Jesus character who's passing right through town. Zacheus was curious about Jesus who stops at the tree. And Jesus is very serious about Zacheus. He is much more than curious. He is very serious. And he says: Do you know what, Zacheus? I am going to dine at your home. I want to sit down with you. I have chosen you who I want to be with.

And that man came down from that tree and he was filled with joy. The encounter with Jesus, the fact that Jesus turned to him in his sinful and hated status, and says: I mean to dine with you. I want to know you. Zacheus was forever changed. That love changed his life forever.

And it is the same Jesus who stops in front of us today, face to face, and looks us in the eye and he says: Steve, I know you and I want to dine in your house. And I want to live in your heart. And I want you to be forever changed because of the love that I have for you.

The invitation is given to each of us. Free to choose, yes. Free to say no. And I would imagine, most of us, if we don't worship once in a while, or quite regularly, it is because we are so clueless of the immense and tremendous and intimate and tender bond that God holds out to us.

I also want to say something else about worship. You can't

know how much it matters to me when you are here. And how I feel it when you're not. The love I have felt for many people in this room who are in my life. And when you are out of town, or whatever, I just feel the absence. I just miss you because a piece of what God gives us is this sacred communion to share. Steve, you touch my heart, and I touch your heart. We are threaded and connected because of the Spirit, because of the love of God. And as we touch each other, we are again forever changed.

There's one rose on the altar. That one belongs for my father, who loved God first, and is with God and in God. But, in fact, this room is filled with millions of roses and their sweet scent this morning.

And each of us is a rose. Each of us has choices to make about allowing God's love to be powerful and alive inside of us or bein' just a little too busy to pray. Too busy to be loved, too busy to worship. Too busy.

Some day, somebody will be standing in the pulpit, talkin' about who gave them faith, who passed that faith on to them, who gave them the great gift, of God's love. Will they be talking about you?

Chapter 14

32nd Sunday of Ordinary Time, November 11, 2001

The vision Jesus gives is a vision with no death, no suffering, no darkness, no favorites, no enemies. We will be, as he said, like the angels.

- Father Greg Tolaas

Gospel Reading

Luke 20:27-38

[27] Then some Sadducees, who say that people will not rise from death, came to Jesus and said, [28] "Teacher, Moses wrote this law for us: 'If a man dies and leaves a wife but no children, that man's brother must marry the widow so that they can have children who will be considered the dead man's children.' [29] Once there were seven brothers; the oldest got married and died with out having children. [30] Then the second one married the woman, [31] and then the third. The same thing happened to all seven - they died without having children. [32] Last of all, the woman died. [33] Now, on the

day when the dead rise to life, whose wife will she be? All seven of them had married her."

[34] Jesus answered them, "The men and women of this age marry, [35] but the men and women who are worthy to rise from death and live in the age to come will not then marry. [36] They will be like angels and cannot die. They are the children of God, because they have risen from death. [37] And Moses clearly proves that the dead are raised to life. In the passage about the burning bush he speaks of the Lord as 'the God of Jacob.' [38] He is the God of the living, not of the dead, for to him all are alive."

Homily

Ibegin with a question for you this morning. A moment for self-assessment. How is your faith? How deep, on this November morning in 2001, how deep is your faith? And your faith? With what faith did you walk into this room? What faith do you need before you walk out of this room today?

We are all hungry for deeper faith.

When I was preparing my homily I threw a whole homily away. I was really hating it and I was sitting in the sun yesterday, kind of by the corner of the garage and I was praying, "God, what was I supposed to say and what's goin' on and all of a sudden, I was very reminded of our parishioner, Howard Brown. You may recall, many of you, that it was a year ago this very week or weekend that Howard Brown stood before our community at age 58, 59, born an American Jew, bright, very smart, medical doctor, anesthesiologist, quite gifted. He had succumbed to cancer, melanoma. And he came with his wife and his children to church here and at one point, he decided I want to be baptized. And he stood in front of our congregation one year ago, with laryngitis, his throat was going; he never did really recover after the day of Baptism, so overwhelmed was he by his baptism. But he stood with a very, very incredible broad toothy smile, and very piercing true blue eyes and he sustained that smile, looking into your faces as you applauded him and welcomed into the Body of Christ, as a Christian member.

Very soon he was again in and out of the hospital within less than three months, he was dead. He who had spent his career as an anesthesiologist, sustaining, literally, supporting life systems, keeping people alive through very complex surgeries, he who was a life sustainer, could not even sustain his own life. And as he was surrendering to the inevitability of his early and young death, unwanted because he loved his wife and his kids and wanted to be alive and here. As he stared death in the face, he had the option to be utterly bitter and be utterly destroyed by death staring him in the face, or to be utterly transformed, full of utter faith.

In the first reading, there are seven brothers. They refused, under the thumb of the Syrian king, to eat pork because it would be the breaking of the law that they lived for. The law of love, the law of Yahweh, the law of God. And they said you can cut our tongue out. You can gouge my eyes out, you can cut my hands off. But you cannot have my heart and my freedom. I belong, not simply to this life. I belong to the king and to the next life. I shall life forever. And my brothers shall live forever, able to laugh in the face of Antiochus Epiphonis, great Syrian king. And they believed, as Jews in this epoch of their history, that we shall live forever.

We come to the Gospel, and the Sadducees sophisticated and educated as they were, did not believe in the resurrection. And so they come to Jesus with this complex thing. We've got the black widow wife here and she marries all seven men, killing them off one at a time. Whose wife shall she be in the next life? And Jesus says, "You don't get it. You always think inside this tiny little box. About wives and husbands and brothers and sisters and who's on top and who's in charge and who has a relationship and who are your favorites and who aren't your favorites.

In the Kingdom, there will be no favorites. In the Kingdom we won't worry who's wife, and who's husband, and who's brother, and sister. Every time we meet one another, it will be love meeting love, and it will be huge, and it will be beautiful, and it will be illuminated, and it will be free, and it will be whole. You won't worry, who's my favorite; who's my enemy, who's on top; who's below, who made it in, who didn't make it in, who's my wife, who's my husband."

The vision Jesus gives is a vision with no death, no suffering, no darkness, no favorites, no enemies. We will be, as he said, like the angels.

Now the fact is, we have faith because faith gives us belief in what is un-provable. Belief in what is un-provable. Howard Brown, for all of his brains, and his Harvard diploma, and all of his education, and avid reader that he was, with an insatiable appetite to learn, and read, and all of his common sense; he was very commonsensical; at the end of all of those gifts, and all of those brains, it was only faith that could cross him into belief. It was only faith that could light up those eyes and give him that smile that says. "I stand in your presence and I believe, despite the cancer ravaging my body, I shall live forever. I shall live forever. That is what faith gave to him. That is what faith gives to us.

Think for a moment, on a broader scale of slavery on this continent. Black slaves. What was it like? What was it like to be born into slavery? To be reared illiterate as a slave? To be worked as a slave? To be bred as a slave? And to die as a slave? Knowing that you never had freedom. Knowing you always took orders from the master? What was that like? And yet out of that very tradition of slavery, came these awesome songs about freedom, these awesome songs, the negro spirituals, as they are called, about I'm gonna cross into Jordan? I'm gonna cross into campground and I'm gonna be free and I'm gonna live forever. And my master's name is freedom and my real master's name is wholeness, and my master's name is Jesus. And I rest in Him. No matter what kind of slave you make me on earth, I am ultimately free. And their very deep and awesome faith gave them, despite the horrors of slavery, gave them a song, and a soul much deeper than my own.

It's funny, we drive in our cars, on the freeway today thinking that we're safe when we're driving. That's a very stupid notion. We are so unsafe when we're in our cars. We go to work thinking that we're going to come home at night. So did the people two months ago today who walked into the World Trade Center, sayin' "Of course, I'll be with my family at the end of the day." We think that we are writing the script for our life. We plan to live well, have good health, live to 95. Then I'll go to heaven.

But the fact is all we have is now. All we have is today. We are no less fragile than Howard Brown. We are no less fragile than the millions who will die in the next 48 hours on the face of the earth.

It is our faith that gives us joy.

Now some of us walked into this room today, perhaps, with casual faith. The casual faith that says, I believe or I don't believe. I'm not really sure; I'm going to think about that later, tomorrow. Some of us in the church, here or throughout the world, we have careless faith. We get to church when we get there. We pray if we bother to. We're kind of into ourselves, our lives, our agenda, our work, our careers, our money, our toys, our drinks.

Some of us have scrupulous faith. We're always in anguish, thinking God can never look beyond my sins and love me into fullness of life.

Some of us have faith nearly destroyed because we've done despicable things, horrible things. And we fail to forgive ourselves, even though God very much forgives us.

And some have an honest faith that says, "I believe God is abundant and good. I believe God loves me and us. I believe in God. I will always be loved."

And some of us have an unbending faith. The faith that says, "I know because of God's gift, because of Jesus' gift, I shall live forever."

Question. How is your faith this morning? What, in your heart, do you know? Are you going to live forever? I am.

Chapter 15

34th Sunday in Ordinary Time, November 25, 2001

Christ the King

He is our life, our bread, our way, our truth. And He says always and everywhere, "Love is enough."

- Father Greg Tolaas

Gospel Reading

Luke 23:35-43

[35] The people stood there watching while the Jewish leaders made fun of him: "He saved others; let him save himself if he is the Messiah whom God has chosen!"

[36] The soldiers also made fun of him: they came up to him and offered him cheap wine, [37] and said "Save yourself if you are the king of the Jews!"

[38] Above him were written these words: "This is the King of the Jews!"

³⁹ One of the criminals hanging there hurled insults at him: "Aren't you the Messiah? Save yourself and us!"

⁴⁰ The other one, however, rebuked him, saying, "Don't you fear God? You received the same sentence he did. ⁴¹ Ours, however, is only right, because we are getting what we deserve for what we did; but he has done no wrong." ⁴² And he said to Jesus, "Remember me, Jesus, when you come as King!"

⁴³ Jesus said to him, "I promise you that today you will be in Paradise with me."

Homily

Many of you have been praying, I hope, and I think, for my friend, Ginny Kelly, who is still alive. Forty-four years old, still the mother of three little girls, dying of cancer, struggling hugely, tremendous pain, but still alive.

I also have a friend, Bill Meerkins. He's eighty-six. He comes every Saturday morning to do my lung treatment. Wonderful guy, charming, warm. He's almost down to skin and bones but he will not miss those Saturday treatments, despite how he feels with his cancer.

And our friend, and my friend, Father Jim Smith, his

mother living with, dying with cancer, has a few months to live.

And metaphoric death; it is all around as well. People living with depression. People caught in the death of addiction. People who have great suffering. One could say: Death is all around us. Any one of us in this room probably could name somebody in our life or in our extended life who is sick, suffering, addicted, depressed, or dying.

Yet we bump into, on this last Sunday of the Church year, we bump into this feast, called Christ the King. Christ the King. And you think of a king. A king, with all of his glory, all of his might, all of his regality, all of his power, all of his prestige. And on Christ the King, what do we hear about? We hear about a homeless carpenter, preacher, who is hanging on a cross, who actually didn't even have a rag around his waist. He was buck naked. This is our king? This is our prestigious, regal, powerful king? What do we do with this king? What do we do with this Prince of Peace? What do we do with this great mistake?

I was reading in a book recently, about an excerpt from Josephus's annals, his writings, in first century. He says Pilate was a cruel man. He didn't just have the crucifixion of three tidy souls up on the cross that we read about today. At one point, Pilate, in a very bad mood, seeing the Jews were being a little restless, insurrectionists, as a matter of fact, political naughty children, in the empire, he had two thousand crucified down a row. And when you were crucified, after the horrific death, by suffocation, and bleeding, and humiliation, you did not have the dignity of having your body taken down from the cross. You were left to be eaten by vulchers and buzzards and wild dogs. It was a statement. It was a reminder: BEHAVE! Or else. And yet, here is our king. A peacemaker, a teacher, known to be a gentle soul, one who was radically inclusive of whomever. One whose identity, and definition and self definition was simply this: Love. Love.

We say, in that second reading, that he was king of the universe. That he was co-creator of the universe. That he was the alpha and the omega. The be-all and the end-all. The king of all kings. But when you really bring it down, he was one thing only. And one thing is enough. He was always all love. And he says to us that the answer is love. He was the voice of God. He was the sacrament of God, the holy sacrament, given to us, God's self in flesh, who at any price, any price, refused to stop loving. And said to us: This is the answer for the world. So I stop for a minute, and I look at our world, and I say to myself, for every century since he died and rose, for every century, there has been war, and more war, and more war, and for some reason, even though his message was radical love, his message was radical reconciliation, his message is that the only freedom comes through love, we insist on wars! We continue to strategize, even in our century, even this week, that the answer must be a military answer. Cuz that's what we know how to do. That's the only thing we can figure out. And I dare say, I don't have the answer, I am not a military strategist. But I am wrestlin' with this: If the Prince of Peace, if the Lord of Lords is all about love, and always about love, then unloving action, is not what he teaches us. It is not the answer.

Different paragraph. I think of the people, the people in this room, the people outside of this room, the people in this neighborhood, the people in every neighborhood, who are struggling with addiction, addiction to what? To sex. Addiction to drink. Addiction to drugs and every kind of chemical. Addiction to work. Addiction to prestige. Addiction to power. Addiction to control. Every family has certain members who are kind of control freaks. I'm a control freak. Somthin' I need to know about myself, so I can work on that. Or we have people who are addicted to being abusive in their primary relationships. We even have people who are addicted to being the victims. They're always the victim. They're always going to be the victim.

Victim is what they know how to be. But whether it's drugs or booze or control or things or work or prestige, or you name it, addiction is always a dance with death. The only addiction we ought to have is an addiction to love.

What if we were addicted to love? I'm not talkin' about feel-good fuzzy-wuzzy warm love, but real, live, love. What if our answers to problems were rooted in real, live, love? What if, in a family conflict, we solved it, not by grudges or silent treatment, but real, live, love? This is real, live love. Always, in every generation, in every situation, his message was err on the side of love. It is the only answer. Look at our history. Look at our neighborhoods. Look at our families.

Love is the only answer.

The fact is every one of us in this room lives with certain darkness, certain depression, certain brand of addiction, certainly, struggles. The fact is every one of us in this room is lookin' at death, maybe not as quickly as Ginny Kelly, or my friend, Bill Meerkins, or Madeline Smith. Some of us are gonna die sooner than others in this room. But death is looking at all of us.

And this Jesus, His fundamental message is: because I

come from love, because I am filled with love, because I am driven by love, because I am imbued with love, because I am constantly blessed with love by the Spirit who dwells in me, I can never die! You can hang me on a cross. You can watch my body rot! But I will never die. Because love doesn't die.

So when we gather here today, those of us who believe, whether we're healthy or sickly, can say to ourselves: if I give myself to love, if I give myself to the sacrament of love, if I give myself to the God of love, I cannot die. I will never die.

Similarly, those of us dancing with addiction, struggles, darkness, depression, control issues, abuse issues, chemical issues, if we say to ourselves: "This is death. I want life." Then choose love, because He is life. He is our life, our bread, our way, our truth. And He says always and everywhere, "Love is enough."

Only when we believe this, and only when we surrender to it, to the great love, and the Lover who loves us, only when we surrender, will we hear and believe His words he says to us this day, "As for me, I shall be in Paradise and this day, you shall be with me."

The Catholic Church of St. Philip,
closed its doors on June 5th, 2011, after 105 years of
service to the Northside community in
Minneapolis, Minnesota.*

*People of the Father Greg Tolaas Fund, pledge to continue
their work, donating all profit from the sale of books and Cds
of Fr. Greg's homilies, to serve the people he loved in
north Minneapolis.

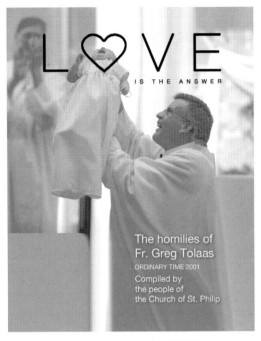

LƎVE

IS THE ANSWER

The homilies of
Fr. Greg Tolaas
ORDINARY TIME 2001
Compiled by
the people of
the Church of St. Philip

The homilies and masses of Father Greg Tolaas have inspired many. For two-and-a-half years, they were put on CD's to share with parish shut-ins. These spoken and transcribed homilies are available from the Church of St. Patrick, making it possible to share Father Greg's inspiring words with his worldwide group of friends.

In memory of Father Greg Tolaas, all profits from the sale of his homilies will be donated to the causes and community efforts to which he devoted his ministry. All labor in the production of this collection is donated, with a great amount of love, by the Church of St. Philip parishioners.

- CUT AND SEND -

SET: "Love is the Answer" book and CDs $45.00
SET 1: "Pay Attention!" book and CDs $45.00
  Postage and handling per set . . . . $ 5.00

SEND TO: (Please type, print, or use address label)

NAME:_____

ADDRESS:_____

_____

CITY:_____STATE:____ZIP:_____

Number of sets @ $45.00 each _____ Total cost_____

  Postage and handling @ $5.00 per set_____

  Total amount enclosed_____

PAYMENT MUST ACCOMPANY ORDER / ALLOW 4-6 WEEKS FOR DELIVERY

Send check or money order to:

The Church of St. Patrick
Fr. Greg Tolaas Book & CD's
6820 St. Patricks Lane
Edina, MN 55439

THANK YOU

To avoid shipping charges, books may also be picked up and paid for at the Church of St. Patrick.

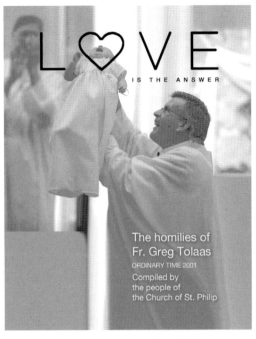

The homilies of
Fr. Greg Tolaas
ORDINARY TIME 2001
Compiled by
the people of
the Church of St. Philip

The homilies and masses of Father Greg Tolaas have inspired many. For two-and-a-half years, they were put on CD's to share with parish shut-ins. These spoken and transcribed homilies are available from the Church of St. Patrick, making it possible to share Father Greg's inspiring words with his worldwide group of friends.

In memory of Father Greg Tolaas, all profits from the sale of his homilies will be donated to the causes and community efforts to which he devoted his ministry. All labor in the production of this collection is donated, with a great amount of love, by the Church of St. Philip parishioners.

- CUT AND SEND -

SET: "Love is the Answer" book and CDs $45.00
SET 1: "Pay Attention!" book and CDs $45.00
            Postage and handling per set . . . . $ 5.00

SEND TO: (Please type, print, or use address label)

NAME:_____

ADDRESS:_____

_____

CITY:_____STATE:____ZIP:_____

Number of sets @ $45.00 each _____ Total cost_____

            Postage and handling @ $5.00 per set_____

                        Total amount enclosed_____

PAYMENT MUST ACCOMPANY ORDER / ALLOW 4-6 WEEKS FOR DELIVERY

Send check or money order to:

**The Church of St. Patrick
Fr. Greg Tolaas Book & CD's
6820 St. Patricks Lane
Edina, MN 55439**

THANK YOU

To avoid shipping charges, books may also be picked up and paid for at the Church of St. Patrick.